AIKI

JOURNEY
TO SELF-MASTERY

by

Bill Sosa

TRAFFORD

Printed in Victoria, Canada

A cataloguing record for this book that includes the U.S. Library of Congress Classification number, the Library of Congress Call number and the Dewey Decimal cataloguing code is available from the National Library of Canada. The complete cataloguing record can be obtained from the National Library's online database at: www.nlc-bnc.ca/amicus/index-e.html
ISBN: 1-4120-1872-2

TRAFFORD

This book was published *on-demand* **in cooperation with Trafford Publishing.** On-demand publishing is a unique process and service of making a book available for retail sale to the public taking advantage of on-demand manufacturing and Internet marketing. **On-demand publishing** includes promotions, retail sales, manufacturing, order fulfilment, accounting and collecting royalties on behalf of the author.

Suite 6E, 2333 Government St., Victoria, B.C. V8T 4P4, CANADA

Phone	250-383-6864	Toll-free	1-888-232-4444 (Canada & US)
Fax	250-383-6804	E-mail	sales@trafford.com
Web site	www.trafford.com	TRAFFORD PUBLISHING IS A DIVISION OF TRAFFORD HOLDINGS LTD.
Trafford Catalogue #03-2250		www.trafford.com/robots/03-2250.html	

10   9   8   7   6   5   4   3   2

I would like to dedicate this book
to my beloved family and
to my many students,
past and present.

Acknowledgments

I would like to thank the Mayans, a wonderful group of people dedicated to the evolvement of mankind. Without their teachings, this book may not have been possible to write.

To Dr. Barry Beaty for the input of his knowledge.

To all my students who encouraged me and have given me their support through the years.

To William Greenleaf for his help and professional advice.

To all of you who have helped behind the scenes and continue to be there for me.

AIKI—JOURNEY TO SELF-MASTERY

Table of Contents

About the Author

Bill Sosa, a 6th degree black belt, is a dedicated and devoted teacher of the martial art of Aikido. He is also founder and director of the International Aikido Association and author of the following books:

The Essence of Aikido with Bryan Robbins,
Unique Publications, 1987

P.A.C.T. Police Aikido Controlling Tactics,
self-published, 1993

The Secrets of Police Aikido,
Citadel Press, Kensington Publishers, 1997

Foreword

Aiki—Journey to Self-Mastery

People have asked me why, after eight years, I am still willing to travel nearly 30 miles from my home or office in heavy, big-city traffic several times a week to go to Aikido class, and then drive the 30-mile return trip. "What about your business obligations, your family activities, your church programs?" they ask. "How do you find the time to do this Aikido thing?"

I responded easily to this question. When I began, the self-defense aspects and the aerobic nature of the training were all contributing in a very real way to my physical development and well-being, and that was good enough.

Now I find it challenging to explain why I continue my training, only because words begin to fail in the face of describing something that is no longer primarily physical. A shift occurred somewhere along the way, a subtle curve in the journey's path.

That change was the gradual realization that I was tapping into something much larger than myself, allowing me to blend with people and circumstances not just on the mat of the training hall. My awareness and control were allowing greater insights into business negotiations, personal relationships, and even spiritual matters. Conflicts could be resolved more calmly, tensions relaxed, stress reduced.

It wasn't about taking a martial art anymore; it was about changing my life.

As my teacher and friend Bill Sosa explains so beautifully in Aiki –
Journey to Self-Mastery, gaining this power over ourselves and responding
to our world more peacefully requires no special tools or permits. For
me, Aikido was the portal providing entrance to the journey. For you, it
may be something different but no less inspiring.

The important thing to remember is that the journey of a thousand
miles begins with the first step, says the ancient Asian wisdom.

So walk forward, and discover a larger universe. The guideposts are
all about you in Aiki – Journey to Self-Mastery.

Tom Eagle
Dallas, Texas

Introduction

"*Aiki*," a Japanese word that translates to "harmony" or "blending with nature," is not a style form or a martial art. It is a principle of energy that holds a powerful potential for individuals to reach beyond the limitations and boundaries of the self. It encompasses the ability to coordinate the mind and body, and to take advantage of every opportunity that could create peace and harmony. This peace and harmony must be experienced by each individual separately, and must come from within. Aiki holds the key to opening the gate that leads to the path of self-mastery.

Before beginning to write this book, I thought long and hard about what title to use and what kind of book I wanted to write. I did not wish to write a book on the physical aspects of Aikido, which derives its name from Aiki, or to give the impression that only those interested in Aikido would benefit from reading the book. While I'm personally very dedicated and devoted to the study of Aikido and its martial application, the Aiki side has a special and attractive meaning to even those who do not wish to study and become proficient in the physical techniques of the art.

Although the body of this book covers the elements that are necessary for self-mastery, and can create harmony and peace in an individual's life, I am including some notes here on the martial aspect of Aikido in relationship to Aiki.

Aikido, the Martial Art

The term *Aikido* refers to a martial art that originated in Japan in the mid-1920's. It was developed by Master Morihei Ueshiba (O'Sensei). Master Ueshiba studied the traditional Japanese martial arts, particularly jujitsu, from renowned masters who taught selected students privately. The skills that he learned had been tested on the battlefield for hundreds of years by Japanese Samurai warriors.

Master Ueshiba was a deeply religious and spiritual man. His practice of Buddhism profoundly affected his philosophy of life and his martial art. As a result, he modified the traditional effective but deadly techniques and martial ways into a new way of self-defense that is effective yet at the same time gentle, loving, kind, and—whenever possible—harmless to an aggressor.

This sounds different from the martial arts we usually see in tournaments and in the movies. In fact, it *is* much different.

In translating the Japanese term Aikido into English, we begin to see the profound differences between Aikido and other martial arts. *Ai* translates as "harmony," *ki* as "energy" or "spirit," and *do* as "the way," loosely coming together as "the way of harmonizing or blending with energy." Thus we could say that Aikido means blending into an aggressor's energy, or even a friend's energy, or perhaps universal energy.

In a self-defense situation, by blending with an aggressor's energy—his strike or hold—and redirecting that energy for one's own advantage, the aggressor is neutralized and can be assisted to the ground into a controlled position. A joint lock or pin renders the aggressor harmless but causes no permanent injury. As opposed to other martial arts, the Aikido student does not take advantage of his control to injure, maim, or kill his opponent. He may use his skills to project the aggressor away from himself so that the aggressor is no longer a threat, but the Aikidoist does not directly block his opponent's strike or clash with his opponent. Rather, he blends with his opponent's strength or *ki* (energy).

Besides being gentle, blending with, and redirecting an opponent's force, Aikido moves are always more effective than physically clashing, especially when an opponent is bigger and stronger. An Aikidoist is never the aggressor.

What I am describing here is a gentle, non-aggressive art of self-defense, one that neither seeks to compete nor to win with brutal force and destruction of others.

In Aikido, the goal is the perfection of character and the unification of mind and body. There are no contests or trophies, as in other forms of martial arts. The challenge is to continually develop technique and spirit in comparison with oneself, rather than with others.

Initially, Aikido students are usually motivated to train by advancement in rank (signified by belt color) and the status that this gives in the *dojo* (training hall). As time passes, the motivation to train changes. Students are motivated by the spiritual aspects of the practice. Ranking becomes secondary.

The spiritual side of Aikido is, in many ways, more powerful than the physical side. Although these two sides cannot be separated, the spiritual side soon becomes the focus of the practice for many Aikidoists. It is this side that is used every day in the fabric of one's life.

Training in the Aikido arts is not just learning throws and pins. The training itself has a much deeper meaning that extends beyond the class techniques. As the student progresses and begins to understand and develop his techniques, he also begins to develop his balance, grace, timing, and self-awareness. The student has a responsibility to challenge himself to a deeper level of study and understanding.

When the physical Aikido arts are practiced with honesty and integrity, this same attitude begins to permeate all the daily activities of the student's life. The student must keep reminding himself of the importance of applying the same principles in daily life if he wants to become proficient in the art. When this is done, the ability to interact with people in a more positive and productive way is increased.

The student can then apply this attitude of blending to other areas in life, such as in negotiating business transactions. Rather than clashing with the other side, or trying to destroy the opponent, a harmonious approach allows for the needs of all to be attained in a mutually acceptable way. Trust is developed, and that leads to more negotiating success in the future. This carries over into other situations, such as in the office, in the home, and even in traffic.

Aikido encourages spiritual growth that strengthens the doctrine of love and gentleness as taught by all the major religions, both Eastern and Western. A new student of Aikido will find himself immersed in a practice of gentleness that is consistent with his religious beliefs.

Truly, Aikido has a special meaning for each of the hundreds of thousands of Aikidoists around the world today. For many, it builds self-confidence and a more secure feeling from physical attack or abuse in day-to-day living. To some, it means an added security that eliminates bad thoughts or gives a more positive and assertive existence. To some, it means leaving an accumulation of anger, resentment, aggressiveness, and other negative baggage behind, enabling the student to channel his energies in a more powerful and positive way.

Aikido is a gentle art of self-defense that spiritually and physically puts an individual in harmony with others when the techniques are practiced on the mat. When students pair off to train, their task is to sincerely find and develop their Aiki, the fundamental principle of blending with the attack.

Aikido is based on the principle that the laws of the universe are in complete harmony. We are all part of this universe, and these laws apply to us as individuals. When the laws are broken, it creates disharmony and brings chaos into our lives.

The Scriptures remind us to know ourselves so that we may be free. It takes time, study, and practice to get to know ourselves and to develop physically, mentally, and spiritually. With age should come wisdom, but this is not always the case. If we look around, we will find this to be true. Many are confused and have no real purpose in life. Others, who are confused themselves, choose to follow someone who is equally confused or misguided.

We should learn to make time to really get to know ourselves. Each individual has a purpose in life. For some, it takes time to find that purpose, but "seek and you shall find." Keep trying. If we die trying, at least we know we went out like a true warrior. Once we give up and quit, we have defeated ourselves and our purpose in life.

With self-mastery, the journey through life can be much more fun, exciting, and rewarding. Try it and see!

CHAPTER 1

Courage, Compassion, and Kindness

On the road to self-mastery are many qualities which the student of life must acquire in order to achieve Aiki. "Aiki" means to harmonize one's energy with oneself as well as with all other energies. Courage, compassion, and kindness are among the vital qualities necessary for reaching the goal of self-mastery through Aiki.

Courage is the mental fortitude and quality of mind that enables a person to meet dangerous situations and opposition calmly and bravely. *Compassion* is the sympathetic consciousness of others' distress, together with the desire to alleviate it. *Kindness* is the state of being forbearing and having a gentle nature that is disposed to be helpful and solicitous to the needs of others.

It is the individual who possesses these qualities that makes an impression on us. We will remember that person forever. We might recall the rough periods in his life when the odds were stacked against him, yet he handled the situation at hand with strength of character and lack of fear.

Several years ago, a marvelous story in one of the Chicago newspapers illustrated how the qualities of courage, compassion, and kindness can meld together in one human being.

One day a sergeant in the Armed Forces was called to the front office and informed that a telegram had just arrived. The son of one of the men under his command had been killed in an automobile accident. He was given the assignment to inform the man of this tragedy.

This was one of the toughest and most painful assignments the sergeant could have been given, to break the bitter news to a parent about his dead child. One can imagine what thoughts must have gone through the sergeant's mind. The task required not only the ability to appreciate the delicacy of the situation, but also to have the courage, strength, and compassion to deal with it.

The sergeant went to the man, called him to his side, and gently broke the sad news. Upon hearing that his son was dead, the man fell to the ground and began to cry.

In the midst of comforting the man, the sergeant was again called to the office.

"A terrible mistake has been made," he was told. "It was not the soldier's son who has been killed. I am sorry to say, it was your own son who has died."

Both the sergeant and the soldier had the same last name.

The sergeant went back to the man, who was still on the ground weeping. "I have good news," the sergeant said. "There was a mix-up. It is not your son that is dead."

When the man heard the news, he stopped crying, wiped the tears away, and began to smile as he was understandably relieved to hear that his son was alive.

The sergeant looked him in the eye, put his arm around him, and with compassion said, "I'm glad your son is still alive."

Obviously, this sergeant's great strength and capacity for love, compassion, and understanding gave him the courage to deal with life's sudden misfortune, and at the same time be of help to his fellow man. He was working in harmony with the energy that was presented to him.

Courage

It takes courage to step out of one's own discomfort or pain and think of others during a time of sorrow and loss. Many lack courage when outside things begin to fall apart. They lose control and fall apart themselves. For those who are not spiritually equipped to deal with adversity, their world simply collapses. They are not prepared for the crisis at hand.

In Carlos Castaneda's book *The Teachings of Don Juan*, the great Yaqui teacher Don Juan tells Castaneda that the task of a warrior is not to hex or charm, but rather "not to crap out." To be in control when everything is perfect and going our way might make us feel powerful and mighty, but it does not require much strength or courage. The true test comes when things are not going right. This is when we find out what we are made of. When we are under the gun, we find out whether or not we have achieved self-mastery through self-control.

Although many situations during our lifetimes will require a serious nature so that responsible decisions can be made, a sense of humor can help to maintain a balanced perspective and lighten the load we carry. Life can be funny at times, and we should all learn to laugh and not take ourselves too seriously.

However, humor has its place and proper timing, too. The person who plays the clown role at all times, and does not know when to be funny or when to be serious, hardly has what is needed in a tough situation. He runs the risk of being taken as a buffoon, which has implications of its own. A person who spends a lot of time being cute and funny never develops the inner strength that is so desperately needed to cope with the serious side of life.

To gain control, and to show courage under adverse situations, requires extensive work and preparation. We need to constantly develop the spirit so that it can sustain us during trying times. Practicing compassion and kindness are two ways that can help to build a foundation for courage during times of trouble.

Compassion

Compassion is synonymous with love and a strong desire for the comfort and well-being of others. It is not only important, but it is necessary that we learn to care for others. The sergeant in the story showed that he had compassion for the man whose son had died, and he continued to show compassion for the man's mistaken grief despite his own deep suffering.

One day while talking to my students about sharing and caring, and how important it is for the salvation of the soul, I asked if anyone had questions.

One of the students arrogantly asked, "Why should we care for others?"

This kind of thinking is prevalent in our society today. With so many diverse groups of people, the most foolish individuals are those who always question: "Why? Why should I bother? I'm only one person. How could I possibly affect the world if I cared?"

If everyone had this kind of attitude, this world would be in worse shape than it already is. This mentality can stunt personal growth and the overall development of a human being. The question should not be, "Why should I care?" but instead should be, "Why *shouldn't* I care?"

If we are not capable of loving and caring for others, how do we expect others to love and care for us? If everyone loves one another and cares about the well-being of others, no one would want for anything. There would be no greed because everyone would receive what they need through sharing. There would be great feelings of joy experienced simply through giving and caring. It would be a beautiful world. By practicing compassion in our own small way, we can experience personal joy, happiness, and peace.

Kindness

Kindness is another benevolent quality. Through acts and thoughts of kindness, we can relate harmoniously to all people in all situations. We have all experienced the gift of kindness from others, which brings a warmth in knowing that someone really cares about us and has our best interest at heart. It feels just as good when we help others. A wonderful feeling arises inside when we are kind to others.

Remember the Golden Rule: "Do unto others as you would have them do unto you." This is a simple karmic law of cause and effect. Our actions, positive or negative, influence that "cause and effect" by the choices we make. If we want others to be kind to us, we must in turn be kind by putting out positive and loving energy.

When one is being kind, he is not judgmental or critical. He is simply expressing interest, concern, and encouragement to his fellow man. When one is being kind, he forgets about himself and thinks about the other person's needs. A kind person looks for opportunities in which he may help others. He does not mind being delayed or inconvenienced, or even sacrificing himself in order to help someone.

I once found myself at the bustling Tokyo station in Japan, where I was waiting to board the bullet train that would take me to Osaka for an overnight stay. Early the next morning, I was scheduled to take a plane to Taiwan, so I didn't have a lot of time to waste.

My ticket for the train ride had been purchased through the hotel where I had been staying. All I had to do was get to the station and board the train. However, for someone who has never been in that station, believe me when I say this: It is one huge place with hundreds of people hurrying in different directions.

My heart was racing as my time ran short. In such a big place, I had no idea where to begin looking for the proper level and the proper track, nor what to even look for, since all the signs were in Japanese—a language I did not speak or read. I was beginning to doubt whether I would board my train on time and reach my destination.

I attempted to get help from people scurrying by. "Do you speak English?" I would ask.

They would shake their heads, or blatantly answer, "No."

I could not remember when I had felt more helpless or alone.

Suddenly, from nowhere, a young Japanese man appeared. He walked up to me and asked in fairly good English, "Can I be of any help?"

After I explained my dilemma, he looked at the ticket and directed me to the proper entrance. I cannot say how relieved I felt. I almost hugged and kissed the man. I thanked him profusely and boarded the train.

This young man helped me for no apparent reason other than that he saw me struggling, and he cared. He showed his caring through his kindness. I didn't get his name, but I shall always remember this gentleman with gratitude in my heart.

We all need a helping hand from time to time. It does not make a difference what our financial status is, or what kind of title we carry around with us. We all have "being human" in common, and there will be a time when we will need someone to come to our aid.

Show concern for others by being kind, regardless of who they appear to be. We should show kindness because we can make a difference and because we want to help. There are many ways we can show love and caring for each other. The stories about the sergeant and Japanese gentleman demonstrate this.

Law of Karma

In order for us to grow as individuals, we must develop courage, compassion, and kindness in ourselves so that we can be useful to our fellow man when he is in need, and at the same time help ourselves in our own situations.

We cannot give something we do not have. This pertains to everything, be it food, money, or love. If we do not have love for ourselves, how can we show love and kindness to anyone else? It is often assumed that if a person loves himself, he is not capable of loving others. This is simply not correct. It behooves us to learn to be compassionate and kind toward ourselves.

The Scriptures tell us, "Love thy neighbor as thyself." This points out the importance of loving ourselves as well as loving others. To love ourselves is not the same as being "in love" with ourselves. Vanity is shallow and has nothing concrete or positive to offer. When we love others and ourselves in the right way, we show gratitude and respect for God's creation and we honor His work.

The law of karma, as well as the Scriptures, teach that, "As you sow, so shall you reap." Again, everything in life is cause and effect. This cannot be overstated. Whatever we think, say, or do, which is the *cause*, creates some kind of *effect*. If we say something demeaning to another, then we create an effect of making the other person feel humiliated, resentful, or angry, and that feeling comes back to us in a negative response. When the young Japanese man in the train station stopped to help me, he created a warm bond of love between us that can never be broken. Through the act of his kindness, the *cause*, he created a lasting *effect* of love for him in my heart.

Karma is the main principle behind all individual responsibilities. It teaches us the importance of realizing that we have control over our destiny through our thoughts, words, and actions. Unless we change our mental habits, which set up the cause, the effects will continue as they are now, so we will remain unchanged and unable to progress.

Mental habits of thought affect the emotions, which in turn affect the body and its actions. By learning to be more conscious of our thoughts, our minds can be a power station that will help us to leave trivial pursuits behind and focus on the true purpose of life, which is to develop ourselves in every way possible.

We can develop qualities of courage, compassion, and kindness by controlling our thoughts, by letting in the positive, constructive thoughts and locking out the destructive, negative ones that sometimes want to control us. When the negative thoughts creep in, we must immediately switch to a happy memory, sing a happy song, or say a little prayer.

Try a positive affirmation. Be selective with thought patterns!

Summary

By showing compassion and kindness to others, and by learning to control our thoughts, actions, and words, we can develop the foundation that is necessary to build the inner strength and courage necessary for harmonious daily activities, as well as dealing with unexpected events. With these qualities in hand, the path to self-mastery will begin to widen and we will soon begin to see the effects of the good deeds that we perform, which can fill our lives and world with joy and harmony.

CHAPTER 2

Mental Power and the Second Wind

God has blessed mankind with an invaluable and precious gift: the mind. If properly developed and used, this wonderful thinking, reasoning, and creative mechanism can lift us to enormous and unimaginable heights on the path of self-mastery. In fact, self-mastery is mental mastery.

Everything starts with a thought or an idea, then the thought materializes. From the tallest, most magnificent building, to the houses we live in, the cars we drive, the clothes we wear, the beds we sleep in, and our favorite chairs—all these things began with a thought. As a matter of fact, we were also just a thought in the beginning.

As individuals, we are the sum total of our thinking habits. The Scripture says, "As a man thinketh in his heart, so is he." Therefore we need to be very careful about what we think and how we think. When a thought crosses our minds, it is registered forever in our subconscious, and later shows up in our actions.

Untapped Mental Power

Besides becoming aware of our thoughts and directing them in positive avenues, we all have resources that are hidden, untapped, and unused simply because we do not realize that we have them. How can we make use of something if we are not even aware that we have it?

When the Scriptures remind us to "Know thyself," and "The Truth shall make you free," they are suggesting that we develop ourselves, discover our capabilities, and use them for the betterment of the world.

When it comes to mental power, all of us are capable of achieving much more than we realize. Researchers tell us that most humans only use about two to five percent of their mental capacity. Taking this into account, there is little wonder why so many fail in their attempts to succeed in life. At the first sign of inconvenience or problems, many people simply give up and quit, or lack the courage to continue. Many feel they do not have what is needed to solve or overcome difficulties in their lives. To these people, quitting and giving up is the easy way out. They move on to the next project, and the same thing happens again and again. Many grow old and die, never achieving anything of significance in their entire lives.

Just think what this world would be like if our pioneer fathers had that kind of mental attitude and had abandoned a project at the first sign of trouble. Not much would have been accomplished, and we would be living in a different world. Instead of driving cars and flying in airplanes, we would still be riding horses and drawing wagons.

Everyone has the capacity to develop themselves and contribute something to the world. I'm sure we've all heard the old adage, "What the mind can conceive, it can achieve." If we learn to think in ways that we thought were impossible, our mental capacity will begin to open up. We all have unused and latent mental faculties that must be opened to prepare us to cope with any situation life can present. On our way to self-mastery, we must strive to go beyond what we believe to be our limits.

First, realize that the mind is not incarcerated in the brain. The brain is similar to a switchboard. The brain is actuated by the mind and, in turn, all body movements are activated by the brain. The activities of the body, spirit, and soul are all directed by the power of the mind. Thus, with correct thinking habits, followed by the proper action, nothing is impossible.

I could give example after example of people who, in spite of tremendous odds against them, called forth this mental power and went on to great accomplishments and success. For example, Thomas Edison failed miserably for many, many years, as well as through many, many experiments, until he finally discovered how to make a viable electric lightbulb. Helen Keller had severe physical disabilities, being both deaf and blind from the time she was 19 months old, but she went on to become a famous writer and lecturer, inspiring others to great heights.

Martin Luther King, Jr. had to overcome obstacles of poverty, ridicule, and prejudice to become a great passivist leader. Christopher Columbus endured extreme hardships on his ship with inadequate and insufficient food, cramped quarters, and the growing discouragement of his men as the long days at sea often seemed to hold no promise of the land he had envisioned in his dreams.

Despite all the problems and the struggles, and possibly even moments of despair, Christopher Columbus, Martin Luther King, Jr., Helen Keller, and Thomas Edison all rose above the odds and obstacles to achieve great accomplishments for themselves and for all mankind.

Clint Eastwood, one of my favorite actors, once wrote for *Parade Magazine* that we need to challenge ourselves. His father taught him that he had to keep progressing or he would decay, that there was no way to just maintain the status quo. Eastwood went on to explain that staying in sharp mental condition requires mental activity just as staying in good physical condition requires physical exercise. If we do not use our brains, they soon begin to atrophy, and eventually the same thing happens to the body.

It behooves us to take stock of ourselves and become aware of how we use our minds and thoughts, and then to challenge ourselves to build a positive mental attitude and reach beyond our limited beliefs of what we can achieve.

Second Wind

Almost everyone has heard about the so-called "second wind," and the vital mental thrust that is derived from it. For example, a long-distance runner, after falling far behind in a competition, comes on strong in the final seconds to win the race. A prizefighter, after being badly beaten, comes out of his stupor and knocks his opponent cold in the final round.

This second wind applies not only to sports and martial arts like Aikido, but to every aspect of our lives, even to our health. I have personally known several people with cancer and other terminal illnesses who lived for years beyond the time-expectancy given to them by their medical doctors. These people simply refused to give in to the doctor's diagnosis and decided to call forth this inner power to live additional productive years.

A young man I know named Randy has a serious diabetes illness. He has needed a kidney transplant and a pancreas transplant for years now. In order to keep him going, surgery has been performed on nearly every part of his body. He has endured pain, treatments, and long and unpleasant hospital stays, yet this young man looks forward to each and every day of his life. He has a wonderful sense of humor and a positive outlook. He just takes one day at a time.

For years, Randy looked forward to his kidney transplant. Now he does not even mention it. He has defied the odds on his life span. As of this writing, five years have passed since Randy was given one year to live. He is still living and doing the best with his situation—a good example of mental power and determination.

As long as we are still alive, we always have the opportunity to turn a situation around. Unfortunately, so many people stop trying when a doctor tells them that the end is near. Others may give in to an old negative way of thinking, and feel it's too late to improve their lives if they are past a certain age. Perhaps they feel their health is too far gone and beyond repair. Others feel they don't have much time left in life, so they say, "What's the use?"

These people neglect to make use of the marvelous power of the mind to step beyond the seeming limitations of their own making, or beyond the findings of someone else. It is never too late to change or try a different way. This can be done by changing our thinking patterns. It is always better to make the best of our lives, not only for the time we have left now, but for the next life to come.

In life there will always be conflicts and obstacles of some kind. No matter how large or small the project we undertake, it deserves nothing less than our best efforts. One of the most common mistakes we make is to give up and quit at the first sign of failure, tiredness, or exhaustion.

In Aikido training, we practice developing the second wind when we do an exercise called *kokyu-dosa*. This exercise is performed with every test criterion for rank advancement. The exercise is always done last, after the student has performed all the different forms and defense techniques required for a test. Depending on the level of rank, a student is usually exhausted by the time he has to perform kokyu-dosa.

Aikido, by its training nature, provides many ways of testing the power and the quality of centralized energy, or *ki*. Kokyu-dosa, however, is by far a much superior test, as the object is to control the situation by moving directly into the line of force without collision or struggle. This exercise not only develops a strong *ki* flow, but at the same time it engages the mental power associated with the second wind.

Kokyu-dosa is performed in the kneeling posture known as *seiza*. By the time the student is finished with all the physical requirements of the test, there is not much energy left. In order to be successful and pass the kokyu-dosa test, the student must reach deeper within himself, so the second wind has to be called forth.

Virtually everything that has been built, whether a truck, car, locomotive, or airplane, has a nominal function and capacity, plus a built-in reservoir of power for emergencies, or for pulling loads much heavier than is usually required. We humans were created basically the same way: energy and power for ordinary living, and reserve power for extraordinary tasks, emergencies, and success. Just as the driver of a loaded truck has to shift down to a lower gear in order to climb a steep hill, we humans also have the ability to shift to the lower gear of reserved mental power. It is the mind that activates both energies in the human.

All men and women who seek true knowledge and success will take advantage of this mighty reserve power on their journey to self-mastery. There is something very positive and exhilarating about the second wind. Not only does it produce a great feeling of power, but the chances for success and achievement are greatly magnified.

Training the Mind

The key in training the mind for both regular activities and the second wind is to learn to be very selective in your thought patterns. One of my favorite sayings goes like this:

Pay attention to your thoughts; they turn into words.
Pay attention to your words; they turn into actions.
Pay attention to your actions; they turn into habits.
Pay attention to your habits; they turn into your character.
Pay attention to your character, because it becomes your destiny.

We should constantly pay attention to our thoughts and make the necessary changes. It has been said that if we can learn a better way of thinking, then we might live a better life. An old Chinese saying reminds us: "If we don't change the direction we are going, we are likely to end up where we are headed."

We all find ourselves indulging in negative thinking from time to time. The trick is to not become stuck and entertain those thoughts for long. When we catch ourselves thinking fearful and negative thoughts, we should make a sincere and strong effort to change them to positive thoughts. It takes practice. But it's that simple.

If we are watching a particular show on television, and it's not to our liking, what do we do? We change the channel. Sitting in our favorite chair with the remote control in hand, we have the power to choose what we're going to watch on the screen or to turn off the TV altogether. When it comes to our minds, we can use our invisible remote control, which comes from our willpower, to choose what thoughts we're going to entertain.

Be aware that negative thoughts can cause us to underestimate ourselves and our potential. Most people think they know their limits. However, much of what they think they know isn't true knowledge, but erroneous and self-limiting beliefs. Self-limiting beliefs can be a great obstacle on our path to success and self-mastery.

The martial arts offer an excellent opportunity to practice ways of training the mind. For example, Aikido places a lot of emphasis on mental training. We realize the mind leads the body; therefore, it makes good sense to train it properly so the body will follow its commands at will. Results and techniques become easier and more effective with practice.

Another important lesson to remember is that things may not always be what they appear to be in the first place. The problem is not always what seems to be out "there," but how we react to what happens. The same problem that turns out to be stressful and monumental to one individual might become an exciting challenge and a learning experience for another. Control and command of the mind to think and act positively will help tremendously to break the negative chain of thoughts that produces stress in the first place.

From time to time, one needs to do an assessment and a complete overhaul on oneself—in other words, to re-examine thinking habits, policies, and ideals. Here, we must consider the way we live our lives, and the things we believe in. Has life turned out well for us? According to our highest standards, do the results turn out to be satisfactory? If not, wouldn't a change be helpful?

Many people are afraid of change, afraid of the unknown, afraid of how events will unfold if they try something different. But remember that change is a universal law. In order for us to grow, develop, and evolve, there must be change. When we begin to realize the importance of change, we will see things differently, and thus do things differently.

For instance, we will start to choose our friends and companions with more care because we will realize that the people we associate with strongly influence us. There is an old adage, "Tell me who you are with, and I'll tell you who you are." When we change our thinking, we can recognize that we have the power to be selective about the people in our lives, and we can choose to associate only with those who will help us grow and better ourselves.

Summary

Each of us should make a strong effort to become thoroughly familiar with the power of the mind and the second wind, and what this can add to our lives.

First, we need to know that we have this capability within us, then proceed to make use of it. Always train the mind in a deliberate and positive way. We have the power to choose and control what goes into our minds. Proper practice will surely bring about good results.

Remember, the path to self-mastery is mental mastery. The mind has no limits. We can be masters of our own minds. All it takes is sincere practice and a strong desire to change. When we find ourselves thinking in a negative way about something or someone, we can either change it to a positive thought, or stop the dialogue altogether.

When we master the art of thinking, we will begin to attain that harmony of spirit that only comes from effort and practice. We will succeed in finding the way and solution to anything and everything. This is the true experience of attaining Aiki, that inner harmony.

CHAPTER 3

Sportsmanship and Self-Control

An important aspect of harmonizing one's inner spirit on the path to self-mastery comes from self-control that is exhibited through one's sportsmanship. Sportsmanship may be defined as "conduct becoming to one who engages in sports or any affairs with other people, particularly where there is some kind of competition." Sportsmanship displays the qualities of one who is fair and generous, a good loser, a gracious winner. Sportsmanship displays respect for other people over and above the desire to win or make a personal gain.

Competition in Sports

It is interesting to note how competitive sports have a way of bringing out the best and the worst in people. We have seen athletes make the sign of the cross or pray before a competition, to ask for guidance, protection, and victory. At the same time, it is quite common to see outbursts of rage, fist fights, and even riots during a sporting event. These encounters may take place among the participants, as well as the spectators.

If you have any doubts about this being true, just watch a hockey game. Good sportsmanship is almost non-existent. It is common for hockey players to spend a considerable amount of time in the penalty box for fighting. Broken noses, knocked-out teeth, and black eyes are all part of the game. A good or bad game is often decided not on the merits of talent, but rather on how nastily the fights are played out.

Although competition can be positive because it can offer a challenge to develop one's physical and mental skills of strength and endurance, quite often, in free enterprise and in sports, the goal of competition seems to be to destroy the competitor.

A few years ago, a professional football coach offered his players cash bonuses to injure and take out the place-kicker from the opposing team. A few years later, the same man was the defense coach with a different football organization. He took a punch at the offense coordinator of the same opposing team. This incident was nationally televised. When asked by reporters why he did it, the coach merely commented, "It's just a difference in coaching philosophy and the heat of the battle."

We all have individual minds, and often think quite differently from others. But does that give us the right to take a swing at someone who disagrees with us? This is where we have to make choices about controlling our emotions and actions, or letting them get the best of us.

Another reporter asked the coach, "Is all this fighting necessary?"

"Emotion is just a part of the game," the coach said self-righteously.

In the meantime, another scuffle erupted in the press box between two other members of the same team. This time the receivers coach and the quality control coach were going at it. They had to be pulled apart.

Many people seem to find this type of behavior in a football coach rather amusing, and they dismiss it as part of the macho game of football. However, if the neighborhood bully broke the arm of a child in a fight, the parents would be terribly upset and would want to do something about it to resolve the problem. But when a grown man, a professional football coach, puts a bounty on someone and pays to have him busted up, the viewers think that is justified, that it adds excitement to the game.

Can we honestly expect more intelligent and responsible behavior from our younger generation than we do from mature adults? Rising teenage violence and crime on our streets and in our schools have become a grave national concern and nightmare. While the numbers on teenage violence in this country should be of great concern to us, that concern should not stop with just the young generation.

If we can't figure out why the nation's youth morality is on the decline, maybe we should take a long, hard look at ourselves: the adults, the parents, the teachers, the clergy, the sports heroes, and the political leaders. After all, we, the adults, set the tone and example. Whether we realize it or not, we serve as role models.

The question is: What kind of role models are we? Do we ever stop and ask ourselves, "What do I really stand for? What kind of lessons do

I teach my kids? Do I encourage them to win at any cost, and that being number one is all that matters?" Could it be that through our own misguided perspective, we not only expect, but demand, that our children be just like us?

Many are wondering what went wrong and what has happened to us as a society. All we have to do is watch a typical hockey game to observe the hatred and violence that runs rampant in the sports arena and is televised around the world. This is absorbed into the consciousness of all those who watch the games, and then spills over into other areas of life as a natural outcome.

Emotions without self-control can be very dangerous and eventually lead to serious consequences. In physical confrontations, just as in war, there will always be the victor and the vanquished.

Competition in Politics

Another area where sportsmanship is sorely lacking is in the political realm. Partisan politics have become increasingly vicious and hostile. It is common knowledge that many well-qualified and decent individuals abandon their well-intended aspirations of serving in government. They have seen the kinds of personal attacks and humiliation they would have to endure, and simply find it not worth their while.

It goes without saying that anyone nominated for government office should not only be well-qualified but should hold up well under scrutiny. The question is: How far should this scrutiny go before it destroys all highly principled and valuable candidates? It is not possible to find perfect people who have not made mistakes.

Society is slowly becoming weary of the so-called "attack-dog" politics and the insatiable thirst for negativism in campaigns. This is a positive direction for improvement, both in the campaigns and in the number of candidates with higher principles who might come forth.

In regard to politics, the news media, with its tremendous power of influence, has a great responsibility to report the truth. In a democratic society such as ours, the best government is still a government "of the people, by the people, and for the people," instead of by a selected few who use the news media to distort the truth and weaken or destroy the political opposition. When the media allow themselves to be manipulated by self-interest groups and individuals, they add to the underhanded, vicious game that defies the rules of true sportsmanship.

The public has a right to expect proper conduct from their elected officials. This same code of ethics should be expected from journalists, citizens, parents, teachers, and all those who serve as role models for our youth.

In the true spirit of sportsmanship, violence and hostility have no place in sports, schools, streets, or in politics. We must all be responsible for our own actions and learn to respect the rights of others.

Violence and Crime

Violence and crime are often used as political footballs by politicians who manipulate votes out of the issues to either stay in office or attain a new position. Yet not much gets accomplished after the voting is over.

For the most part, no one seems to know what to do about violence and crime. Some propose building more prisons. Others propose handing out stiffer penalties. Still others seem to think putting more cops on the streets will resolve the problem.

While it is obvious that more prisons, more cops, and stiffer sentences are indeed needed, are we foolish enough to believe that these in themselves will take care of the problem? None of these resolutions will have a lasting benefit because we are treating the *effect* rather than the *cause*.

Unless we change our thinking and actions, unless we learn to take control of our emotional responses to others in competitive circumstances, as well as teach our children how to do this, we will have to continue to build more prisons and put more police officers on the streets. The only sure change we can expect from our current mentality will be the amount of tax dollars we, the public, will have to pay.

History has already shown us that the possibility of going to prison is not an effective deterrent to hatred and violence. The fact that jails and prisons are so densely populated proves this point.

Prison Inmates on the Rise

According to the U.S. Department of Justice, Bureau of Justice Statistics, the number of jailed Americans is on the rise. At the end of 1999, the incarceration rate had more than tripled since 1980. 6.3 million people were on probation, in jail or prison, or on parole at the end of 1999—

3.1% of all U.S. adults. Between 1990 and midyear 1999, the incarcerated population grew an average 5.7% annually.

It seems clear that the threat of going to jail or prison has little effect on the sick and confused criminal mentality. For many criminals, serving time is considered a great badge of honor among peers.

On top of that, most habitual criminals are very familiar with the law and know how easily it can be manipulated in their favor. The revolving door policy of letting inmates out as fast as possible to make room for more is a pathetic joke at best. While the police are catching and putting criminals in jail, judges and parole boards are letting them back on the streets just as fast, often with only a slap on the wrist.

Our prisons are full of individuals from all walks of life. Some are hardened criminals with minimal hope of rehabilitation. Others have been misguided by circumstances in their lives. And some were even unjustly incarcerated. While there should be a place or system in which criminals pay their dues to society for their actions, it should also be a place of education.

It is foolish to think that just because someone has served his time, he is going to behave once he is released, especially if the individual doesn't have anything to look forward to. Once released, most former inmates have nothing waiting for them on the outside.

The prison system, while still a place for punishment, should incorporate a mandatory program designed to teach inmates trades and skills, as well as offer job opportunities once they have served their time. Unless we prepare them to blend into society and become useful, most of these individuals will wind up in prison again.

No plan is going to work one hundred percent of the time. So while some ex-convicts are going to have a tough time adhering to a proper code of conduct, some will be willing to amend their negative prior lifestyles if given the opportunity and necessary skills.

Education and Role Models

Educating ourselves and our children is a start in the right direction toward eliminating violence and hatred. Education comes in different forms and should not be viewed only as traditional school learning. While traditional schooling is very important and necessary, the other form of education pertains to ethics and moral principles that lead to the building of good character and conduct. This kind of education would have a positive impact on everyone. We as individuals have a responsibility to live our lives with integrity and awareness. We also have a responsibility to teach our children these greater values.

One day a student of mine in his early twenties asked to speak with me in private after class.

"I have a serious problem with my father," he said. "I want some advice from you because I don't know how to handle this myself. My father is a retired military man, and he wants me to follow in his footsteps. He wants me to join the Navy, become a Navy Seal, and make a career of the military just like he did. I am aware of the role I'd have to play as a Seal, and this is troubling me very much because I do not like violence. And I also believe in the way of Christianity.

"I am aware that not all Christians are conscientious objectors, yet I believe that a true Christian does not have to adhere to killing or violence. I want no part of it."

"Did you speak to your father about this?" I asked.

"Yes," he said. "When I told him that joining the Navy is not in my best interest because of my own religious beliefs, he became very angry and reminded me that he had been a good Christian all his life. He said that serving in the military was part of being a good American and a good Christian, and my lack of interest in the military was un-Christian, un-American, and un-patriotic." The young man paused. A look of sadness and uneasiness shone in his eyes. "I love and respect my father very much. I am torn between wanting to please him and doing what I feel in my heart is right." He then looked me in the eye and asked, "How do you think I should handle this?"

"My advice to you is to follow your conscience and your heart. But I also think you should talk to your father about his feelings on this. You need to explain to your dad that your lack of interest in the military has nothing to do with patriotism, being a good American, or being Christian. Tell him you would like to do something different with your life. You may want to tell your dad that you do not wish to sound disrespectful, but you would, in all probability, not make a very good Seal if your heart was not in it and you joined just to please him. Tell him you believe you will be more useful to the world when you find a career that you like and that brings you satisfaction."

In this situation, the father used his own biases and authority to try to influence his son's will and destiny. To make his son feel guilty and accuse him of being unpatriotic and un-American because of his lack of interest in the Navy was not only improper and unethical, but also shameful and dangerous. It showed not only a lack of understanding and concern for his son, but a lack of intelligence as well.

A father's role with his child should never be one of dominance and control, but rather one of guidance, understanding, and support. It is our obligation as parents to help our children in every way possible. To help them choose a way of life or career is important, but to impose our will on them because of parental authority and power is simply wrong.

Religion, Peace, and Love

Christianity is sometimes used by people as an excuse for manipulating their children, spouses, friends, and relatives into doing things their way. Christianity is used by others as an excuse for not taking control of their lives and improving themselves. Many people go to church, to a synagogue, or to a mosque and really believe they are serving God. But serving God can too easily mean being intolerant of those who do not believe the way they do. In this sense, religion is used as a means to justify hatred and judgments of others.

I once heard a popular and respected minister on television ask, "Do we go to church on Sundays because we are seeking truth? Or do we just go there to rearrange our prejudices?"

We may go to church on Sunday and tell ourselves that we are good Christians because we are serving the Lord, but if someone rubs us the wrong way, watch out, because we will see that the person gets what is coming to him—in the name of the Lord. Do we really believe this is the way God wants us to serve Him?

Good religion is good relationships with people—all kinds of people. Good religion projects itself in caring for others and in sharing with others. Good religion is a way of life that does no harm and does not demand its rights at the expense of others. This type of religion is more akin to what Christ taught. And this is exactly what good sportsmanship means.

Those who believe their hatred is justified because of religion, patriotism, or race, do not understand the true nature of God. Our God, the Intelligence of the universe, wants us to love and care for each other, sharing the abundant wealth of the universe. For instance, many would agree that peace is worth dying for, but Christ taught that peace is worth *living* for when He said, "Blessed are the peacemakers, for they will be called the children of God."

Some people claim they want peace so badly they will fight and kill for it, which is the irony of it all. Some believe they are "fighting for God," and think that it's great to go to war and avenge injustice and achieve peace in the name of God. In Ireland alone, masses of people have been murdered in the name of religion. The Catholics and the Protestants each promote their religious beliefs, failing to comprehend the true teaching of Christ. Lasting peace will never come about through fighting, killing, and destruction.

Life is short, and we never really know what the next moment will bring, or if we'll even be around. So while the opportunity exists, it is important that we strive to learn all we can and always do our very best. We must cultivate our minds so we can obtain wisdom and share it with others so that we can contribute something positive to the world.

True victory is achieved when we find peace within ourselves. This peace will come when there is a change of mind that causes us to do the right things. For example, if we support the idea that because there has always been war, there will always be war, nothing will change. Indirectly, we are still supporting the war mentality. If we vote for politicians and world leaders who are eager to go to war instead of going to the negotiating table, then we ourselves are supporting war.

Do we really want to believe this is the way it has to be? Is it really true that history has to repeat itself? Could it be that we do not learn from our mistakes and fail to use the wisdom of hindsight? Someone once said, "If we're not careful, we'll go back to the Stone Age mentality. The difference will be that, instead of stoning each other to death, we'll just blow up the entire world with nuclear arms."

True peace has its foundation in love, and we must learn to love one another even if we don't like each other very much. There are times when, as parents, we may dislike our children for something they do or do not do, but does that mean we stop loving them? In order to grow and have peace, we must use the principle of love toward one another. We were created by the same Creator, and that in itself should encourage us to love each other.

We say that we want peace among nations, and quite often we don't even have it at home. Either we don't think it is important enough to do something about making peace, or our pride is so overpowering that it just will not allow us to think in these terms. We might say to ourselves, "Let him come to me and apologize if he wants to be friends, because I'm not about to do it myself." Self-importance, or ego, is an extremely heavy load to carry, and one should seriously consider how long he is willing to carry this load if he ultimately wants to find true peace.

The smart and alert person not only learns from his mistakes, but sees the benefit of learning from others' mistakes as well, and adjusts his life accordingly.

Law of Karma and Free Will

This brings us back to the law of karma. This law of cause and effect never fails. If you do not learn from your mistakes, you will continue to suffer. If you do evil things, then evil will certainly find its way back to you. If you do good, then good will come to you. That is the law.

The kind of energy we put out will dictate the kind of energy we will receive in return. As long as we live our lives with attention and awareness, we will find this to be true. If we take something that does not belong to us, watch and see if we do not lose something of more value in return. If we hurt someone, we will also be hurt. The payment is not always with material things. Sometimes it is much worse: an accident, sickness in the family, etc. The reimbursement process usually doesn't take very long.

A minister friend of mine once told a story about another minister who had just returned from a funeral service for his son who had died in an automobile accident.

After the service, the minister was sitting in his den, understandably sad as he contemplated the event. A lady friend, wanting some advice, walked into the room and noticed his sadness and pain. She stopped and decided not to approach him at this time. Instead, she remarked out loud, "Sometimes I do not understand the will of God at all."

When the minister heard her remark, he jumped out of his chair and grabbed her by the arm. He looked her squarely in the eye and said, "That's right, you don't understand the will of God at all. I just buried my son today, and I'm hurt and I'm sad, and I will miss him terribly.

"But let me tell you something about my son. He was twenty-four years old and he was very irresponsible. He usually drove his car too fast. He also liked to drink and drive at the same time. He never bothered to keep his car in good running condition. Chances are, he was driving too fast when he lost control of his car and wound up in the bottom of the lake.

"You see, God gives us maximum freedom with limited protection, and that means we must learn to be responsible for ourselves and the way in which we live." He paused for a moment and relaxed his hand on her arm. "God had nothing to do with my son's death. His death had to do with the careless way in which he lived his life."

It is clear that God created the human race with the freedom and power to choose. We are created in God's image, with a mind and a will. This will is the strongest force in the universe. God wants humanity to do what is proper and correct, not out of necessity, but out of intelligence. We have free will, so we can decide to choose right or wrong, love or hate.

Unless we are from a different planet, it is universally understood that we are human. It is also understood that as humans we are not perfect—but is it enough to know we're not perfect and just let it go at that? Some people will readily argue and point out that we're only human and it's natural to err. While that may be true to some degree, how many of us continue to use that line, over and over again, as a crutch because we have no intention of changing our ways?

Along with being human comes a moral obligation to improve ourselves. While God is very patient with us, I don't think it is wise to continue to test His patience with the attitude that because we're human, that in itself should be sufficient. That doesn't sound like wise judgment, and I sincerely doubt that God appreciates it.

More than Christianity

It is not merely enough for one to proclaim that he is a good Christian simply because he goes to church on Sundays. To be a good Christian means to be a reflection of Christ and what He lived for. To be a good Christian means to show it in the way we live our lives, in our actions, and in the way we deal with our fellow man. To be a good Christian means one needs to develop Christ-like qualities of knowledge, tolerance, love, and compassion for one another.

We need to learn how to heal ourselves both physically and spiritually, and we must come to terms with our often distorted and hypocritical views of hatred, racism, and violence. We must, in all honesty, seek truth every waking moment of our lives so we may learn to become free from the bondage of ignorance that is responsible for much of our suffering. We must become one with Christ so other people will not only feel it, but they will see it in our actions.

Ultimately, to be a good Christian means practicing the principles of good sportsmanship, good will, and love in all our affairs. If we are to be totally honest for just a moment and ask ourselves, "Do we sincerely qualify to call ourselves a good Christian?", what kind of answer would we get?

Summary

God did not create us as robots, so we as humans have the power of choice. We, the human race, are the descendants of a true King, God, and part of our royalty is the freedom and power to decide and choose our own paths. We can choose to express ourselves through judgment, hatred, and violence in order to try to prove ourselves better than others, or we can learn true sportsmanship through self-control by expanding our outlooks to encompass the value within all persons, no matter what their race, sex, culture, or beliefs.

By educating ourselves and our children, by practicing self-control in competitive situations, by showing respect for the rights of others, and by taking a solid look at ourselves and where we can change for the better, we not only become positive role models for our youth, but we move closer to the love and peace that we seek on the path of self-mastery.

CHAPTER 4

Faith and Success

In order to succeed at anything, we must first believe that we can do it. We must have faith in ourselves. In other words, "What the mind can conceive, the mind can achieve." This includes having the faith that we can attain self-mastery through study and effort.

Faith

Faith is "a strong expectation for something desirable." It has courage at its root, and leads to victory. Faith, like everything else, can be developed. Where there is strong faith, there is no room for fear.

Albert Schweitzer, German missionary and Nobel laureate, once said, "Man must cease attributing his problems to his environment, and learn again to exercise his will—his personal responsibility in the realm of faith and morals."

Faith depends on a positive attitude that says "Yes!" to life and embraces the opportunities life offers for learning and growth. This almost always requires patience and persistence, especially when starting something new. The challenges are harder when we're embarking on a new project or idea or skill because we don't have experience to fall back on. But with practice and determination, we can get better and better, and soon we look back and see our progress, which gives us encouragement to keep going.

We should understand that we're going to experience disappointment and become discouraged at times. It's only natural to have doubts when we begin new projects, but that shouldn't stop us. As long as we keep working toward our goals, we'll notice improvement. As long as we keep developing an awareness of our habits and thoughts, and keep applying the principles of self-mastery, we will reach our ultimate goals.

Another way to understand this is to think of ourselves as carpenters building a house. The house must have a firm foundation and strong framework or else it will not stand for long. We must work each stage very carefully, making sure that we have done our best work without trying to rush it along, only to find that we have left out something important along the way. Even the largest houses and the tallest buildings are built one piece at a time. As we work toward self-mastery, remember that every action we take is building a piece of our future.

Facing the old habits that keep us from reaching our potential is another problem we will encounter. We simply must accept that we can go beyond anything we've thought or done in the past, because until we believe we can do something, we'll never try. What any other human has done, we can learn to do, too, as long as we have faith, believe in ourselves, and make a sincere effort to accomplish our goals. Believing puts us in a proper and receptive frame of mind, and makes learning much easier.

In the *Power of Myth*, Bill Moyers asked scholar Joseph Campbell how ordinary people—those who are not poets or artists or who have not had a "transcendent ecstasy"—can develop an understanding of deeper truths. Mr. Campbell responded, "Sit in a room and read and read and read, but read the right books by the right people."

The old saying that the best-educated person is the self-educated person holds a lot of truth. It may be that the self-educated person is never totally satisfied with what he's been taught in school, so he makes the extra effort to learn all he can on his own.

Many "educated" people have knowledge about certain things, but no wisdom or common sense to apply it. Wisdom comes from making the best possible use of the knowledge that we have acquired so that we can continue to learn.

We live in a world that is changing rapidly, due largely to the alarming rate and growth of the human population. Along with this growth, new challenges, as well as opportunities, present themselves. Our commitment to ourselves and the world is to become as knowledgeable as possible so we can help ourselves, and at the same time acquire a growing mind that will enable us to help one another.

Solid thinking can lead to solid living. It's important that we learn to translate learning into proper living. We must have faith in ourselves to become successful at proper living.

Success

Being successful means different things to different people. To some it might be financial independence. To others, it might be the accumulation of material goods. To still others, it might be social acceptance, or spiritual development.

A person might very well consider himself successful if he has great friends, a wonderful family, a job, and physical health and strength. Perhaps he has achieved a high level of knowledge and wisdom and is truly grateful, satisfied, and at peace with himself. Certainly all of these qualities and achievements are of great importance and would put anyone into the category of success.

One thing is certain: everyone wants to be successful at something. To learn more about how people view success and what it takes to attain it, we might try this experiment. Ask several people at random if they would like to be successful. The answer will probably be, "Yes, sure, I want to be successful."

Then ask them what they are doing to attain success. You will find that a very small percentage are actually stepping out of their comfort zones and doing what is required to bring them success. Furthermore, if they are asked what they would have to accomplish to consider themselves a success, they will probably give vague answers.

Most people relate success to having money, or the ability to make a lot of money. Material possessions and financial status have become the standards for the measurement of success in our society. Quite often, we adopt these standards without even being conscious of what part they play in our lives. The trick is to not become trapped by such standards.

Since we live in a material world, there is nothing wrong with material desires, and money is obviously necessary. But material wealth should not be the only goal. Many times the major aim in acquiring money is not the money itself, but rather what can be acquired with it. The money is then used to get something else that is desired.

God wants us all to be successful and contented. There is nothing wrong with having nice things, if you so desire. Desiring material goods is not harmful in itself. However, on the path to self-mastery, it will soon become obvious that while material goods can be useful and necessary, they do not show the way to inner peace and true happiness. Satisfaction in life is of paramount importance to those striving to master themselves, and we must learn to judge correctly what will give us true and lasting satisfaction.

Knowing What We Want

If we want to achieve anything in life, we must know what it is that we want. We need to find out what we are best suited for and develop along those lines. Whether we are aware of it or not, we each have a purpose in life and a responsibility to better ourselves in every way possible—physically, mentally, and spiritually. Knowing what we want from life, and what we are good at, is part of the journey toward self-mastery.

Not many people really know what they want. They go through life not knowing why they are here or what their function should be. They never get around to giving the subject any deep thought. How can they ever expect to succeed or achieve goals if they do not know what they are doing here, or cannot identify those things that they desire? And many of those who do think they know what they want usually do not really desire what they think they want, because they never make any effort to attain it.

If we want to know the answers to our desires and direction in life, we need to go inside ourselves. In the quietness of our own thoughts, the answers will eventually come. We must specifically ask, "What do I really want out of life? What do I really want to do?" We must be very honest and sincere with ourselves. Soon a picture or a thought will become clear in our minds, and we will know exactly what it is we are here for, or what we want to achieve, or what we desire.

When the image becomes clear, we must take the proper action and do whatever is necessary to go after it in a more direct way.

A young student of mine once said, "I am not getting from Aikido what I feel I should get. What kind of martial art do you think I should study?"

I asked him, "What did you expect to get from your training in the first place?"

"I don't really know. I just know I am not getting it from Aikido."

I appreciated his honesty. He was a very young man who was searching, but he did not know what he was searching for. I responded by saying, "It is just as difficult for me to advise you and tell you what other martial art you should study, when you yourself do not know what you really want from your training. My advice is that you meditate on what you are looking for until you get the answer. Once you get the answer, find the proper school, enroll, and make a strong commitment to stay with it until you get the results you want."

Just like this young man, there are countless numbers of people who do not know what they want from life, or how to start looking for it. They will join this or that group, hoping to luck out and find the one thing that will make them happy or bring them success. This haphazard process is pretty much like throwing darts in the dark at a target one cannot see.

True success is not merely getting what we want, but knowing what it will mean to us after we get it. What part will it play in the overall scheme of things? Is it right for me? Will obtaining what I want be considered the ultimate success? Will it bring happiness and satisfaction? We must each find out for ourselves, and then make a commitment.

Passion, Purpose, and Self-Discipline

Despite the fact that we find many people who live their lives without any spark or enthusiasm, we also find people who live their lives with great passion and purpose. When people like Benjamin Franklin, Michelangelo, Albert Einstein, Charles Lindbergh, Eleanor Roosevelt, Babe Ruth, Kevin Costner, and Michael Jordan realize their purpose in life, they pursue it with passion, enthusiasm, and energy. They do not take a backseat attitude because they are so immersed in what they believe they can achieve. It takes a dedicated and strong-willed person, one who is willing to withstand opposition in life, to succeed.

The list of truly successful people who made it in spite of many failures and setbacks is quite long. Few, if any, can claim their road to success was smooth, easy, and free of difficult demands and hardships.

We can learn from these highly successful individuals, from athletes to martial artists, from musicians to scientists, from physically-impaired individuals to doctors. Almost all who succeed in accomplishing something great will tell us that the most important factor in their success was self-discipline. They train themselves to stay focused on their ultimate goal to the exclusion of everything else, and they will not allow obstacles to hold them back. These people realize that self-discipline is mental discipline, and they waste no time on trivia that could hamper their success.

44

Thus, the key to success in anything we set out to do is self-discipline. Self-discipline, for most people, is not only considered difficult, but also viewed as self-denial. As a result, it is looked upon as a negative quality connected with inconvenience, struggle, and conflict. But self-discipline need not be negative at all. It can be turned into a strong and positive force for change and accomplishment.

We must learn to trust ourselves and be willing to change. Even when we think we are satisfied and doing well, we can always improve. If we want to succeed at the goal of self-mastery, we can never stop learning and improving. There is no way one can overdo self-mastery, or reach a saturation point with it. This is a journey that never ends.

Remember, if there is no change along the way, things will simply stay as they are. At one point or another, everyone must become a "gambler." Chances have to be taken in order to move forward. With risks come new opportunities, and from new opportunities come change. This is an ongoing process that never stops. But all the while, the journey gets more exciting and compelling, driving us forward.

We can learn to know ourselves through clarity of mind and by paying close attention to our actions. Ideas come from the mind. When these ideas are put into action, they result in the physical manifestation of the thought. The more positive and beautiful the thoughts we feed the mind, the quicker our mental habits change. Our actions follow accordingly. This is when we begin to make real progress.

Managing the Business of Life

To achieve self-mastery, we must learn to take full responsibility for our actions. The business of life and living is the greatest gift God has bestowed upon us. Do not treat it lightly or carelessly. It is a great challenge and opportunity to grow, learn, and become the best that we are capable of becoming.

We are all in the business of living. People often think that being a business person is restricted to someone involved in a commercial enterprise, such as buying and selling a product or service. Whether or not we are engaged in buying and selling, we are still involved in the business of living. Whether or not we own a business, have an office, or are the CEO of a large corporation, the business of living should take priority over everything else.

How we manage and live our lives will eventually determine our success or failure in everything else we do. How we manage and live our lives will mean the difference between being happy or unhappy, healthy or unhealthy, successful or unsuccessful. The way we manage and live our lives will someday become our destiny.

The person who manages the business of life well has a better chance of becoming successful than the person who does not. There is really no one else to rightfully blame if things do not turn out right for us.

From the day we are born, we have a responsibility to life, and that responsibility is to do the very best that we can in everything. A true warrior always seeks *impeccability*, which means "being free from fault or blame" or "being flawless." By living our lives impeccably, we will be fulfilling our responsibility to life and living a deeper and more meaningful existence in society.

If one wants to live a good, strong, and successful life, then one must learn effective and practical ways of dealing with the everyday matters of life. A sloppy, careless, and aimless person does not make a good candidate for the simple job of sweeping the floor, much less the president of a company. Just as a commercial business cannot expect to operate successfully without proper and orderly methods, so too, our lives will not improve unless these same methods are applied.

The business of living requires care and organization to become profitable and successful. It is not merely enough to go to college, get a degree, and find a well-paying job to call ourselves successful. To tend properly to the business of living takes careful planning. It takes action. And above all, it takes consistency and determination.

Training in life management skills is not only required to live successfully, but it is seldom taught in colleges. One area of training that needs attention, but is sadly neglected, is the area of productive use of time.

We have all heard the old phrase, "I was just killing time." First, we cannot *kill* time. It would be more appropriate to say, "I am just wasting time." Second, wasted time produces nothing of value and is lost forever.

Time is precious. If used wisely, it allows us to improve ourselves and to achieve our goals. There is truth in the sage advice, "If you need help with something that has to be done now, ask a busy person." Idle people tend to procrastinate, or to make excuses that they do not have time to help us because they are watching television or involved in idle chit-chat. On the other hand, busy people somehow find time to get projects done despite heavy schedules. They function in an efficient mode and get results. They realize time is precious and they don't waste it.

The winners in life do not mind hard work in order to accomplish their goals. The words "can't" and "procrastination" mean nothing to them.

Indecision and procrastination go hand in hand. We must be deliberate and give serious thought to all decision-making. Not being able to make up our minds and putting things off indefinitely are a waste of time. They keep us from accomplishing our goals.

Many people make life more difficult by putting added pressure on themselves through confusion and procrastination. They go through life making the same mistakes again and again because they fail to see who they are and what they can become. Life for them becomes a monotonous, boring routine, a series of motions performed automatically day in and day out. This state of existence can only produce negative, unhappy results.

We must become clear about what we are going to do and, based on that clarity, decide what method of action we are going to take. Then we must do it. We must not allow ourselves to hinder our progress with limiting thoughts. One of the most common errors in human endeavors is not realizing one's own ability and potential. We will never know what our capabilities are until we try them.

Success is Unlimited

There is no limit to the level of success a person can obtain when the proper methods are learned and applied. First, we have to do away with the poverty-stricken and limited mentality that so many people seem to have. Adopt an *I-am-unlimited* mentality instead.

Stop and reflect. Take a moment to ask, "What do I want out of life? What have I accomplished in life? What can I do to help improve myself so that I may help others?"

It takes effort to start a new way of life and to keep it going once we have started, but it is by no means an impossibility.

People often do not realize how hard they work at something that pays absolutely no dividends. Many practice frivolous behavior and use priceless time and energy on matters that are of no importance to anyone. Others make no real effort to find something better to do, or to discover what they are best suited for. For instance, in many cases much time, talent, and energy are devoted to crime, whereas if the same energy were applied to an honest and legitimate endeavor, outstanding success would be the result.

We sometimes encounter what are called "the friendly obstacles." Many times what appears to be an obstacle in our way is actually an ally in disguise. These allies could well be considered guardian angels, since their main function is to save us from ourselves.

At times a friendly obstacle is placed in our path to warn us that this is not the right path. We should then take a different route, because the one we are on will not pay good dividends in the long run.

The secret here is to learn to distinguish the difference between a friendly obstacle and a plain obstacle. They are all great teachers, since their purpose is to teach us to survive. Each obstacle solved will be a step closer to success and self-mastery.

On the road to self-mastery, we have much to gain and nothing to lose. Even if we try something that does not work, we must look at it as a temporary setback and not a failure. Someone once said that success is only a series of setbacks. When we try something that does not work, we still come out ahead because we have gained an education. We find out what does not work and we try a different method. Thomas Edison's success with the invention of the lightbulb came only after many failures—all of which contributed to the foundation which eventually led to success. All problems present opportunities to allow us to make assessments and to learn what is needed in terms of the action we should take. Each problem will be unique, requiring a special approach.

We can do ourselves a big favor by not thinking that we are unfortunate, or victims of circumstances, when difficulties or obstacles get in our way. Instead, we can think of the difficulties as a challenge and an opportunity for learning and growth.

There is always something worthwhile to learn from problems, if we will only allow ourselves to be receptive. How do we accomplish that?

First, we must learn to believe that we have what it takes to overcome any problem life has to offer. Secondly, we must see that all the energy, effort, and mental power we have to call forth in solving these temporary setbacks will bring out the best in us and make us stronger. If we honestly and sincerely appraise the problem before us, then we will clearly see what has to be done. Once we see what we must do, we must tackle one problem at a time until it is solved.

Some people feel a need to be envious of those who are successful, who have plenty, and who seldom encounter major struggles or problems in life. It is wrong to be envious of anyone, and when we indulge in this emotion, we are attracting more negative energy our way.

We should always be glad for someone when they are doing well, and sincerely wish them the best. In the end, we always reap what we sow, and that includes how we think and feel toward others. When we feel good or happy for others, then we will feel good about ourselves. "Love thy neighbor as thyself" is one of the greatest lessons in the Scriptures, and one that we truly need to understand and practice daily if we want to be successful in all ways.

If self-satisfaction is lacking in our lives, then personal reflection is necessary. Each of us is an individual with strong and weak areas, but remember that each of us is also gifted in some way. We must find out what our gifts are and start to develop them. Keep in mind that the results will be proportional to the amount of effort we exert.

The saying goes, "It is better to fail trying, than not to try at all." In the long run, those who try, and keep trying, do not really fail. In life, everything comes with a price tag. The question one must ask is, "How strong is my desire to succeed?"

Nothing that is of value should or will come easily. Someone once said, "We are either in a problem, coming out of a problem, or heading toward one." So congratulations! We are part of this great human race in which no one escapes difficulties.

Summary

We must make up our minds that we are going to do everything within our power to attain whatever it is we desire. In order to accomplish this, we must:

- *Determine what we want and where we are headed. A true sense of ultimate purpose in life is essential.*
- *Believe in ourselves and in our goals. Without faith, we will not make an attempt to move forward on our ideas or desires.*
- *Develop our habits of thinking to keep us from limiting ourselves in achieving those goals. The mind can create or destroy, depending on what we choose to think and act upon, so the mind must be developed through awareness and self-discipline.*
- *Be willing to do the required work and make the required effort. This is the only way we will achieve results.*

Results will come if we are consistent and determined to succeed. It will not be quick or easy. Nothing that is worthwhile comes easy. And if it does come easy, we will not appreciate it in the same way.

Be patient, but stay on the path. The results will be positive and the success will eventually come. Each will achieve the victory that is desired.

CHAPTER 5

Overcoming Fear

Fear is our greatest enemy. On the path to self-mastery, it is the one element that can stifle our growth and prevent us from experiencing the deep inner harmony that connects us with our own energy and the energy of the universe.

We all experience fear. It is a part of life that no one escapes. Nonetheless, fear offers us the opportunity to grow, to learn, and to develop ourselves.

Accumulation of Fear

It has been written that humans are born with only two fears: the fear of noise and the fear of falling. These are provided by nature as a means of self-preservation.

As we grow older, we accumulate other fears, and they manifest themselves in many disguises. Some of us fear the past, the future, old age, disease, the opposite gender, new experiences, failure, the unknown, death, etc. Fear is often just a *thought* in our minds that makes us afraid of our own capabilities and actions.

There are normal fears and abnormal fears. A normal fear may occur when we are caught in a heavy storm while driving, with no place to stop or seek shelter, or when we are startled by someone sneaking up behind us. The fear is there to warn us that our lives or health may be at risk. However, when the storm subsides, or when we notice a friend standing behind us, our fear disappears. The fear had a purpose, and it was temporary.

Abnormal fear occurs when we let our imaginations get carried away with negative thoughts of what *might* happen. So much energy goes into these thoughts that eventually they can become reality. Although it is quite natural for everyone to experience fear, it is not natural to live in a perpetual state of fear. To live in constant fear can, and will, have adverse effects on our lives, our health, and our overall success.

Fear, like everything else, starts in the mind. The more we dwell on thoughts of fear, the worse it becomes, until finally we have created our own reality. Fear, in essence, is having faith in the negative.

At its worst, fear is such a powerful and negative emotion that it can paralyze us and bring about the very thing we dread the most. One of my students told me about something that gives credence to how we can attract problems because of our fears.

"I drove to a shopping mall and could not make up my mind where to park the car," she said. "I was driving a brand-new automobile and was afraid it would get hit. I would park in different spots, but none of them felt quite right. None of them appealed to me. Finally, I decided to park next to a trash dumpster, thinking the dumpster would provide a protective shield to my car. While I was shopping inside the mall, the dumpster truck happened to come by to pick up the trash. As the dumpster was raised to unload the trash, my car was hit on the side, resulting in considerable damage."

The woman dwelled so strongly on the negative potential that her car could be damaged, that she attracted and produced the very thing she didn't want to happen. We can get rid of our acquired fears in instances like this by replacing our negative thoughts with positive ones.

In order to eliminate abnormal fear, we must not give in to the fear when we set out to accomplish something. Every time we proceed to do what we feel we must do, regardless of the fear, we become stronger, both mentally and spiritually. By the same token, every time we shy away from performing or doing something because of fear, our spirits grow weaker and weaker until they eventually die. We all know what happens to those whose spirits have died. They also die.

Facing Fears

Many fears are unwittingly instilled in us in one form or another by parents, teachers, caretakers, or anyone who has had an influence on us in our early years.

A former boxer once wrote about his struggle to overcome his fear of not being in control. He called the struggle "taming the beast inside."

The emotions that go with violence—the slow-burning hatred and explosive anger—usually are symptoms of fear: the fear of getting hurt or losing control, or losing a competition. In a game where one gets paid for succeeding at violence, emotions can get out of control. These emotions are often nurtured by outside influences.

In the case of the boxer, as a child he was praised by his mother for killing a bee that had stung him. Soon he was chasing and killing insects for the joy of it. This extended into other areas of his life. Growing up in the streets, he became associated with fighting and violence. Finally, in the ring, he had to learn to control his anger and fear in order to gain the advantage.

Over the course of his professional career, he had learned to contain the violence in himself and was never again tempted to return to the ring after he had left it. He learned to contain the fear that was "out of control" inside himself.

The fear of failure—of looking foolish or embarrassed in front of others—has kept many people from learning, developing, and improving themselves.

One time I asked a talented Aikido student if she would help by participating in a demonstration we were having.

She replied, "I would rather not. I don't think I can do it. You see, I'm so afraid I will mess up."

This form of fear is dangerous because it hinders a person's progress and keeps one from discovering and developing one's true potential. The fear of failure has kept many talented people from realizing their dreams and attaining success. Talent alone is not enough, as this young woman demonstrates. Unless there is strength of character, integrity, and the will to succeed, one will not recognize and overcome one's fear.

On the other hand, sometimes the will to succeed and the courage to step through one's fears can bring about positive results even if the talent or qualifications appear to be lacking in an individual. For instance, in order to be an effective president, whether of a company or a country, a person needs many positive qualities. Courage and determination should be at the top of the list.

It was written in the newspapers that at the time Bill Clinton got into the presidential race, some thought he was not the most qualified person for the Democrats. They claimed there were others with better qualifications who could run for president of the United States. But if Mr. Clinton was the only one courageous enough to accept the challenge of taking on an incumbent president at the height of his popularity, would not this act alone make him the most qualified?

What good is a great-looking résumé or an impressive background if a person does not have the courage to stand up for what he believes? What good is knowledge if one is afraid to take a chance and put it to use? The one who steps through fear to reach his goals is the one who has the best chance to succeed at anything.

Recently, there was an interview on television with a young lady of 17 or 18 years of age, the only female in a group of flying trapeze artists. The interview dealt mainly with the trapeze artist's training program, diet, and lifestyle. But toward the end of the interview, the reporter asked, "Do you consider yourself a brave person?"

Without hesitation, she replied, "I must be, because every time I'm about to go on the flying trapeze, I'm scared… but in spite of the fear, I do it anyway."

This demonstrates courage in a person. To be courageous means one can perform in spite of the fear one is experiencing.

Although courage and confidence are very important, one must be careful to not get overly confident or cocky. A friend of mine once told a story about a professional speaker who earned big money with his lectures.

"I would always get nervous before going on stage," the speaker said, "but I always prepared well, and my talks usually turned out fine.

"One particular time, though, I was not nervous at all and felt very confident, so I decided I did not have to prepare. I had been doing lectures for a long time, I reasoned, and it usually turned out well for me. That night I stepped on stage and bombed big-time."

When the speaker lost his humility and decided to take his performance for granted, he lost the power to make an impact with his lecture. On the other hand, when he was nervous before a lecture, he did not allow the fear to prevent him from performing, but instead used it to force himself to take the proper action and make the appropriate preparation. Fear can be a tool to improve ourselves, as long as we do not allow it to paralyze us.

Anger and Hatred

Repressed anger, shame, hurt, insecurity, and confusion can all contribute to our fears. At times, fear is so deeply rooted it becomes hatred.

Some years ago, as I was waiting for my car to be serviced, another man who was also waiting struck up a conversation with me. He noticed that my vehicle was a Japanese-made car. He remarked, "I would never buy such a car."

"Why not?" I asked.

"It would be unpatriotic because of what the Japanese did to us during World War II."

I responded calmly, "My purchase had to do with personal taste and economics, and nothing to do with patriotism. The war with Japan took place long ago, and America and Japan are now at peace with one another."

"I don't care," he replied angrily. "I hate the SOB's because a member of my family fought in that war and had an arm shot off."

"The bombing of Hiroshima," I pointed out, "also caused a great deal of suffering and damage to the Japanese people."

The man glared at me. Then he clenched his fists, turned, and walked away. As I watched him walk away, I felt sadness in my heart for him. From the appearance of this man, it was obvious how long-embedded hate could cause destruction to his health and spiritual well-being.

We must learn to go beyond the superficial physical action and get to the deepest levels of our fears. In doing this, we must examine our spiritual practices to see if we are addressing them properly. The source of our fears can sometimes be obvious, such as being in a threatening situation. But most of the time our fears are deeply rooted in our subconscious, and they can go all the way back to infancy or childhood prejudices.

Fear of God

One of the most astounding fears placed before us is the "fear of God." Many so-called men of God preach that we should fear God. They say we must live in constant fear of God; otherwise, we are not good Christians. If we're going to fear something, it should be fear of ignorance, not of God.

Along with this, many sincere Christians live in a perpetual state of worry about themselves, others, and the world in general. Worry is an extended form of fear.

It can be very misleading to listen to preaching that instills fear of God into us. It makes it sound as if God is our enemy: pettish, vindictive, and just waiting for us to mess up so He can clobber us. But God is not like that at all. God is an omnipotent spirit that gives life to all His creation. Therefore, God would be the last one we should fear.

God has His laws, and these are the true laws of the universe. He also gives us free will so that we can make our own choices. We're responsible for those choices. If we do not learn to observe and live within those laws, then we suffer and bring punishment upon ourselves.

God is Infinite Love, Wisdom, and All-understanding. When we fail and make a mistake, He is always ready and willing to forgive and give us another chance to learn.

I once read a sermon written by a Christian minister. He wrote that Reinhold Neibur said that the problem in America is not atheism. It's not the God that we do not believe in, but the false god we believe in. It's idolatry.

The minister went on to explain:

> So often, you and I traipse around thinking we've got to convert people because they do not believe in God. God is not the problem. It is the ridiculous and atrocious picture of God that we believe in that is our problem.
>
> Somebody becomes converted and is sincere, but is sincerely wrong. So what do we do? Because somebody is sincere in their beliefs, we let them tell us the way God is. No, atheism is not the problem.
>
> I'd rather have an honest, knowledge-seeking atheist any day of the week, one who wants to find truth, rather than a converted Christian who is wedded to the false interpretation of truth. It's not the God you do not believe in that hurts America; it's the wrong concept of God that you believe in that is hurting us.

In our ignorance, we complain and blame either bad luck or others for our misfortunes. At times we even blame God. But the truth is, God is not in the business of dispensing bad luck. He is a loving Father to all His creations, just as parents have love for their children. Sometimes parents are unable to prevent the negative events that befall their loved ones because of the choices that the loved ones make.

Summary

Fear is man's natural enemy, since it is one of the first things we learn in life. But we can turn that fear into something very positive for ourselves. It teaches us to look at ourselves and find out what is wrong and what we must do to correct it.

In order for us to deal with fear effectively, we must find out what it is we are afraid of. This requires total honesty with ourselves.

Once we realize the cause for the fear, the next step is to remove the cause. For example, one way to cure fear of public speaking is to learn to speak in public. It requires study and preparation, but it can certainly be done.

Aiki, the road to mastering ourselves and attaining harmony of spirit, will be filled with opportunities for us to gain control of our lives and go beyond the point of fear. There will be no limit to what can be accomplished, providing the necessary action is taken. By conquering fear, we develop strength of character, a better self-image, and the qualities possessed by those we greatly admire.

CHAPTER 6

Dealing With Crisis

Along the path to self-mastery, we will often feel that we have things under control through our thoughts and actions. We will feel some certainty of who we are, what we are doing, and where we are going. Events will run smoothly and efficiently.

Then something unexpected will arise to test our inner strength, our goals, and our purpose. These are points of crisis.

Crisis

The word *crisis*, from the Greek derivative *krisis*, means "to examine" or "a turning point." So we could say that a crisis is a critical point in our lives that needs to be examined. It needs to be examined so we can take the proper course of action in accordance with the facts found.

We need to realize that no one is immune to crisis in life. Neither should we adopt the attitude that we have been singled out for more than our fair share of problems. To entertain such thoughts can lead to a morbid mentality and self-pity that may be very disruptive—or at minimum, accomplishes nothing of real value.

At one time or another, almost everyone will experience some sort of crisis. As a matter of fact, the certainty of crisis in our lives is the one true tie that binds all humanity into a brotherhood.

We must learn to be responsible in taking care of problems as they come along so they do not pile up on us. Some like to complain and talk about their problems all the time, while others simply deal with the issue and go on with their lives without getting rattled. Remember that things are usually not as serious as they first appear to be.

The following verse puts crisis very nicely into proper perspective.
God grant me the serenity to accept the things I cannot change,
The courage to change the things I can,
And the wisdom to know the difference.
- Anonymous

The key here is "the wisdom to know the difference." Sometimes things just go wrong that are totally out of our control. We have no choice but to accept them. Other times, we should have the heart and courage to stand up and say, "This is not right, and I think I can make a difference and help change it."

There are also times when we allow minor losses and setbacks to affect us in a negative way, and we lose control of our emotions. This is when we create crisis by our own doing, rather than having it imposed on us from outside circumstances.

Some time ago, I became acquainted with two simple little rules that have had great impact on my personal life. Rule number one: Don't sweat the small stuff. Rule number two: It's all small stuff.

I do not want to give the impression that I am making light of our problems, because we all run into crises of a serious nature. But remembering these two rules has helped me to keep a clear head in dealing with life's many uncertainties.

Putting Things in Perspective

In order to liberate ourselves, we must first learn what is significant in our lives and what is not. Once we realize that there are situations that are either out of our control, or that no longer have importance, we can cut the ties to them.

In the book *Long Live the King*, a biography of the late movie actor Clark Gable, there is an interesting story of an incident that took place in his home. One day a six-year-old boy was playing with a toy car in the study of Mr. Gable's house. The boy found a funny-looking statue on the desk that made a perfect target for his car. He played with the car and statue all afternoon.

When it was time to leave, the boy decided to ask if he could take the target home. He carried the statue to Mr. Gable and asked, "Hey, you want this thing?"

Gable looked down at the child and blinked at the sight of his Oscar in the boy's hand. Then he smiled and said, "No, you can have it."

The mother, visibly embarrassed, said, "Clark, don't be silly." She turned to her son. "Put that back where you got it."

The boy looked from Clark to his mother, and back again.

Gable shook his head and said to the boy, "No, no, you keep it." To the boy's mother, he added, "Earning this was important, but keeping it is not."

As everyone knows by watching the Academy Award presentations, the meaning of an Oscar to an actor or actress is extremely significant. Most actors would put up a spirited fight if someone banged up their Oscar or tried to take it from them. Obviously, Mr. Gable realized at this point that the Oscar was merely a symbol of his accomplishments that no one could take away from him.

The fact that Gable didn't have to think about it, and made a spontaneous decision to let go of an important material object, is very admirable.

School of Life

The school of life is mainly one of crises and learning to overcome them so that we can live positive and productive lives. This may sound strange to some, but we should feel honored that we experience crises. Life would lose much of its meaning and value if all roads were smooth, and life was handed to us on a silver platter. If everything were given to us just for the asking, not only would life become boring, but we would fail to develop as individuals.

Rest assured, though, that God does not overload us with problems. When He tests us in the form of a crisis, it is because He knows we can handle the situation and benefit from the experience. Real progress is made when we learn to profit from our trials and tribulations. This is part of our self-education and leads to new knowledge that will enhance our lives.

Ignorance is the root of all evil, and we are born to learn many lessons and live a good, strong life. When Christ was being crucified and spoke the words, "Father, forgive them, for they know not what they do," He was saying, "These people are ignorant and do not know the true consequences of their acts."

Knowing ourselves is vital, not only to our success, but to our spiritual health as well. We must strive to know ourselves in order to take control of our lives. How can we make positive decisions and cope with life's crises if we do not know who we are or what is important in our lives? How often have we picked up a newspaper and read about a jilted lover or spouse committing murder and/or suicide when a relationship went bad? To others, life is simply not worth living when they lose their beloved possessions. Sadly, they believe that death is the only way out. The precious gift of life loses all meaning to them.

Keep in mind that if too much importance is attached to the unexpected negative situations we encounter in life, it will exhaust and weaken us. Problem-solving requires mental strength and a clear head so we may decide the proper course of action to take.

Just as a hitter in the batter's box sometimes gets a hit, other times he strikes out. As most of us already know, a career three-hundred hitter in professional baseball not only commands respect, but the ability to make big money. Certainly, a hitter of this caliber fits the category of success, and most baseball organizations would not mind having a few of these hitters on their rosters. But what some people do not realize is that in order for a batter to reach the respected level of a three-hundred hitter, he will fail to get a hit seven out of every ten times he goes up to bat!

We, too, should adopt the batter's attitude. "I did not get a hit this time, but I'm going to get another opportunity to try again. The next time I'm going to bear down and try harder." Sometimes we are going to miss. Sometimes it may appear that we are going to be defeated, but this may very well be preparation for victory the next time up.

Many Kinds of Crises

There are many kinds of crises in our lives. For instance, although most everyday decisions are quite common and rather easily made, there are some really tough ones which have far-reaching consequences that can affect other people's lives. This I call the *crisis of decision-making*. Decisions of this type require not only delicate soul-searching, but the courage to act accordingly.

Then we have the *crisis of disappointment*. We have all had plans carefully made and expected a certain outcome from them, only to have things not turn out exactly the way we had hoped. Perhaps we had planned a picnic at the park in late summer, but a sudden downpour with strong winds prevented us from having that pleasant luncheon in a warm, sunny spot. Our crisis was to come up with a new set of plans, such as having the picnic indoors at home, or postponing the picnic until another day. With the crisis of disappointment, we have to learn to adjust, or make new plans, or set up something different for the next time.

Another common event for most of us, which relates closely to disappointment, is the *crisis of frustration*. We might have struggled and given our best effort to something, only to have it result in what seems to be failure. With this crisis, we are usually baffled, but not totally defeated. This feeling of frustration can sometimes be a blessing in disguise. It gives us an opportunity to step aside and evaluate other possibilities.

I would like to share a story about an experience I recently had. With my Aikido workshops, I frequently travel by plane. In all my years of flying, I had never been bumped off a flight. I am one of those individuals who would rather be early and wait for a while rather than have to rush or be late. I like to be at the airport at least an hour before take-off time.

On this particular day, I had already finished my workshop and was returning home. Due to unexpected events, I arrived at the airport only about fifteen minutes before departure time. I learned that the flight had been oversold, and I was not able to get a seat assignment. The next flight out was not scheduled to leave for another three hours, and the airport was located in a small southern Texas town in the middle of nowhere.

I was tired and I just wanted to get home. But when I saw my plane take off without me, I realized I had only two choices. One was to get angry and take it out on the ticket agent, since he was the only employee there. I could put up a good argument and make a fool of myself. The other choice was to simply remain calm and wait for the next plane. Luckily for my health and blood pressure, I made the latter choice. I figured the only thing to do was to put those three hours to positive use and catch up on some reading.

As I stood in line at the ticket counter to make the necessary arrangements for the next flight, an irate passenger who had been bumped off the same flight complained to the ticket agent. The man was not happy about the situation, and he made it clear to everyone.

After finishing my arrangements, I met the man again at the restaurant and we sat at the same table. By this time, he had cooled off and turned out to be a friendly person. We talked for a good while. He said he had been very frustrated about not reaching his destination on time, but decided to calm himself down when he saw that I did not get upset about being bumped off the flight. Since he was rather busy being upset, I had no idea he had paid much attention to me.

I am sharing this experience with you to illustrate that we really never know who's aware of our attitude and actions. How we respond to a crisis can inspire someone else to take the situation in stride.

A step beyond frustration is the *crisis of defeat*. This can have a different outcome for each individual. It may come in the form of overwhelming frustration, failure, or ruin, or all three combined. At times, by our thoughts and actions, we may even cause our own defeat.

Think what would have become of Abraham Lincoln if he had accepted his many defeats and not pursued his goal. President Lincoln, more than any other president, went through severe and humiliating political defeats before he was nominated as the sixteenth president of the United States. Lincoln did not have formal schooling, and yet he would not allow this to defeat him. He was self-educated. His dream was to become a lawyer. As no one would hire him, he studied law on his own and was determined to obtain the higher education needed, regardless of the hardships he had to endure.

After completing military service, he decided to enter politics. Running for the Senate, he was defeated by a large majority. He then became a storekeeper. His store went bankrupt. It took seventeen years for him to get out of debt.

All this time, he never stopped dreaming. He had the urge to go back into politics as a candidate for Congress, and he won by a thin margin. When he ran for re-election, he again faced the humiliation of defeat.

He was turned down and refused repeatedly because of his lack of education and his poor background. Despite the odds, he maintained his courage and again ran for the United States Senate. Everyone, including his family and friends, ridiculed him. Again he was defeated.

At a political convention, he was nominated for vice-president. However, an unknown political candidate beat him in the final ballot. He suffered defeat after defeat, but he never gave up hope. He did not indulge in his failures, but more intensely pursued his ideals until, at the age of 50, he became the president of the United States. He is known in history as the "legend" of presidents.

When we have worked hard and have prepared ourselves, and still don't win, the experience can be invaluable. It teaches us to overcome and survive a loss, and to know that the loss is not the end of the world.

It teaches us to know that we may still achieve victory the next time if we prepare even better, or perhaps try a different strategy. We are never totally defeated until we give up.

Another form of crisis is the *crisis of temptation*. Who has not experienced temptation? When we were born, we were given a beautiful vehicle, the body, to work and play with. Along with this body come desires and frailties that we have to learn to cope with and control. It is when our body's desires overcome our mental strength that we lose control.

No one is perfect, and as human beings we have many weaknesses and desires, as well as opportunities to go astray. Practicing self-discipline and staying on the proper path by not giving in to temptations and appetites can become a crisis. This is a tough one to master, but one that is very worthy of acknowledgment and compliance if we are going to succeed on the journey to self-mastery.

The *crisis of death and sorrow* is one of the biggest challenges that we face in life. We somehow must learn to endure pain and find peace in spite of the suffering. This type of crisis has to be met with an understanding of the true nature of life and death, and we must cultivate faith, trust, and respect for God's will, and accept the fact that we are all mortals.

Death is as natural as life. But if we were to ask someone, "What is the worst thing that could happen to you?" the person would probably answer that it is death, or the death of a loved one.

To some, death is an unpleasant thought. But we must come to realize that nothing lasts forever. Everything that lives—flowers, vegetables, insects, birds, and humans—will die. Nothing survives. That's one of the great truths we must learn to accept. Self-mastery requires facing this truth so that we can rise above the fear of death. This includes the fear of losing others through death, as well as dying ourselves.

We should not look at death as something tragic. What's really tragic and sad is to die without realizing our true purpose in life. Most people do not live up to their potential. They never really take the time to discover who they are and how much they could contribute to the world. We were born into this world to learn how to live, and most of us fail miserably.

Personally, I believe that the spirit and the soul do not die. We are reborn and return in a different form, in what we call a "body." If we do not learn the true meaning of our existence according to this belief, then we will have to come back and suffer again and again until we do learn. The average person either doesn't realize this or refuses to believe it. We think that when we die, we are either going to heaven or to hell, and that is the end of that. We do not realize that heaven and hell also exist right here in this life.

Some people make their own hell by choosing to live a life of denial, always running from responsibility. They are unable to face ordinary, daily problems and use exhaustive excuses to avoid changing their lifestyles. They actually spend more time and energy thinking of ways to get out of matters rather than solving them. Most of their frustrations and crises are of their own making, and are so unnecessary.

This is a difficult way to live, since nothing positive comes out of this attitude. These are generally people with very negative attitudes who constantly complain. Their outlook on life reflects their attitude.

Despite the fact that there are many negative people around us, we can learn something from them: how *not* to be. Many of these people would rather die than change, and consequently they go to their graves unchanged.

Another aspect of the crisis of death is the fact that we don't know exactly when we might die. An example is a relatively healthy military man who was preparing to retire from the service. He had to submit to a physical examination before he could leave. While in the hospital, he underwent the routine tests and was given a clean bill of health. However, on the night before he was supposed to be released to return home, he died of a heart attack.

We must be conscious of the fact that death could be just around the corner and may tap us on the shoulder at any time. Suppose a man plans a long trip and sees that all the necessary precautions for his car are taken in order to avoid mishaps along the way. He has been responsible. Halfway to his destination, he is involved in a fatal car accident. He never reaches his destination, but the fact remains that he assumed full responsibility for his actions up to the moment of his death. And it turned out to be his last and final act on earth.

Now take the same circumstances with a different person. He knows it will be a long trip, but he doesn't bother to have the car checked. He handles preparations for the trip like he handles most matters in his life: carelessly and foolishly. Then his brakes fail and he becomes involved in a car accident that takes his life. His irresponsibility actually brings on the accident.

We often do not realize the seriousness of our actions until it is too late, or when we see how it adversely affects us and many others along the way. We must be responsible for our actions and answer for them.

Ultimately, there is no power on this earth that can help us at the moment of our death. Just as we are born alone, we will die alone. We must begin now, not tomorrow, to reassess our lives and to get them in order, because tomorrow may never come.

Victory over Crisis

Although we have no choice as to when we will die, we do have control over our attitudes, which can make a difference in changing our destinations and even increasing our life spans. Take, for example, the true story of a terminally-ill cancer patient who had been told by his doctor that he was expected to live about six months and would have to have continual chemotherapy during that time. One can imagine what a serious crisis this must have been.

However, the man's will to live surpassed the doctor's diagnosis. Seventeen-and-a-half years later, at the age of 73, he is doing exceedingly well without the need for chemotherapy. His appetite is good—perhaps even better than before the diagnosis, because now he appreciates each meal. He had to slow down his pace and learn the benefits of relaxation and proper rest. He does not spend his time idly, but keeps active with his yard work and a part-time job. He is probably living more now, and enjoying life more at this age, than he was prior to the diagnosis of cancer.

If this patient had been weak, had believed the doctor's words, or had not been able to see beyond the initial crisis, he would have been another statistic six months after the diagnosis. He would have resigned himself to his fate and given up. On the other hand, what we have here is a person's strong will to live and a positive attitude that allowed him to pass through the crisis and survive with poise. This shows his mastery of himself.

In addition to the specific crises that I have mentioned, there are numerous other kinds of crisis such as illness, financial loss, accidents, and divorce. We have all encountered various crises in our lives, and each experience has taught us something valuable to prepare and strengthen us for the next time.

One thing is for sure: no one is alone in dealing with problems. If now and then we miss or make a mistake, we should not allow it to defeat us because it is not necessarily a failing or final grade. Our lives will pretty much be determined by how we meet and handle our crises. Victory is not merely getting what you want or winning over someone; rather, it is self-control derived from the wisdom of conquering the greatest enemy of them all, which is within ourselves.

One day while driving my car in the city, I saw a blind man attempting to cross the street in front of me. I stopped and offered him a ride. He readily accepted. I inquired where he wanted to go and, as we headed toward his destination, we began to talk. He told me his name was John Tapner.

I became fascinated by John's quick wit and sense of humor. He told me he was twenty-eight years old and had been totally blind since the age of fourteen. He had been shot in the temple by his own mother because, as he put it, "Me and some of my friends were horsin' around in the house and makin' too much noise." His mother was trying to sleep off a hangover. She got angry, picked up a gun, and shot him through the head. His life was spared through surgery, but he lost his eyesight.

I was amazed by John's great attitude toward his mother and life in general. I asked him, "What's your secret?"

He replied, "I put the past behind me and keep a positive attitude. I look forward to a brighter future because I know and have faith that the Lord is watching over me at all times."

Then he recited this beautiful poem which he composed himself.

"For you, my heart with love does yearn to bleed,
For indeed it is your cherishable love I do need.
I do raise my very wholesome praise unto you because I know our
    biggest award
Is eternal salvation through our dear beloved Lord."

Summary

We can all use a higher dose of moral courage and faith in dealing with life's adversities. No one is going to be spared crises on the path to mastering oneself, but through self-knowledge and handling daily affairs to the best of our abilities, we will gain strength to deal with unexpected frustration, disappointment, and loss. Beyond this, we must also develop faith in believing that God knows what is best for us and that, ultimately, everything is going to be all right. When we have learned to do our very best in everything and leave the rest to God, the Great Architect of the universe, then we have found the answer to meeting all crises bravely.

We will have made another great stride on the path to experiencing the full glory of Aiki and internal harmony.

CHAPTER 7

Meditation and Ki (Deep Breathing)

On our path to self-mastery, it is very important to learn to breathe correctly, because on this journey we will require lots of energy. One of the best ways to energize ourselves and create a healthy body is through *ki* breathing exercises.

Ki is a Japanese word that means "energy." When we practice *ki* breathing, we cleanse and "energize" the body. All the true masters of martial arts and Yoga, as well as dancers, singers, and great athletes, know the benefits derived from proper breathing methods.

Ki breathing and meditation can go hand in hand. We can learn to relax and prepare ourselves for *ki* breathing. Meditation is a great way to start.

Meditation

Meditation is being in the here and now, living in the moment. It is a simple exercise that we cannot over-develop or over-practice. In that sense, it is not easy. It will seem demanding because there will be times in our lives when we have ups and downs, and will want to set meditation aside until things have smoothed out. This is when we will need it the most, to help us ground ourselves from daily challenges. And we must make the time for it if we want to achieve a higher level of consciousness.

Effective meditation requires discipline. It is a good idea to do it at the same time every day when one first begins. Think about meditation as food for the spirit and soul. Just as we eat on a regular basis to nourish the body, we must not neglect to develop ourselves spiritually through the art of meditation. Although it does take energy to meditate, it is one of the greatest gifts we can give to ourselves.

As with anything we take up in our lives, think of meditation as a daily journey and a personal investment in the spiritual self, because we are, in fact, more of a spiritual being than a physical being.

Anyone can meditate if one chooses to make the time for it. There is nothing mystical about meditation. It is a simple practice of listening to the energies around us, and of stopping the incessant internal dialogue within. When the internal chatter ends, so do judgments, expectations, and ego.

Meditation might be described as a pleasant, peaceful, painless feeling, a sense of wanting for nothing. It is as if we withdraw ourselves from the outside world, and yet at the same time are in the world in a more aware state.

Meditation is practical. It can be practiced anywhere. We can do it standing, sitting, or lying down.

It is impossible to meditate when the mind is tense and active. In other words, the mind has to be "deactivated." Sometimes this is called a state of "no mind" or "empty mind." The Japanese term for "no mind" is *mushin*, meaning "clear mind" or "no thought."

If the posture is slumped, the mind is too passive. The proper posture is to have the feeling of "being in a state of grace." It is a feeling of dignity. It is the intention and the attitude that give the body the appropriate posture.

All the truly great athletes have one thing in common: the ability to quiet themselves at any given moment. These athletes understand how to enter that space of silence so necessary for them to perform at their best. They do this in the midst of a noisy crowd, or in spite of what the spectators are doing.

One of the main principles of the art of Aikido is relaxation. It stresses the coordination of mind and body in all activities. The same principle that works for Aikido can work for us in our daily lives, even if we're not involved in any kind of martial arts training.

We should train ourselves for a state of mind that is completely mindless. By this I do not mean that we are unaware of things. In fact, this kind of discipline makes us more aware of everything around us, since the mind is not cluttered up with thoughts. This also brings about a deep silence.

There is much value in the theory that "silence is golden." There is a definite power and vitality that goes along with it. All the great teachers have realized the true power connected with silence.

I once knew a high-level executive who practiced meditation regularly and had it down to a science. No matter where he happened to be, if he felt pressure building up inside him, he would excuse himself, find a relatively quiet spot, and spend a few minutes meditating. He always returned refreshed and in total control of himself. He knew exactly what to do to let go, and to get rid of the worthless, excess mental baggage that people carry around with them at any given moment.

In order to concentrate properly, the mind must be quiet and cleared so that it becomes receptive to one's commands. The individual who trains himself in this manner soon learns the importance of precision, the result developed by a clear and positive command of the mind. Of course, one does not have to be involved in martial arts or any type of athletics to practice meditation. Anyone can derive great benefits from this practice, regardless of what they do for a living.

Life, with its many struggles and challenges, can at times be very trying and exhausting. This is where meditation can help tremendously.

Learning to Relax

Nervous disorders are common, especially in our Western society. Medical figures indicate that between 60 and 70 percent of all medical ailments are directly associated with the nervous system. Most doctors agree that stress and tension are major contributors to disease.

We live in a stressful society in which meeting deadlines is the order of the day. We go from one hurried, stressful situation to the next, and we tell ourselves that we need to do things this way in order to be successful. But success will not mean very much if we do not have our health to enjoy the success.

Many take their work home with them, along with all the problems associated with their jobs. There is a time to bear down and take care of business, and there is a time to let go, relax, and recharge the system. When we meditate, for instance, the battery is recharged.

Doctors may tell us to slow down and relax. Families and friends may remind us of the same thing. We know we should relax, but quite often the problem is that we do not know *how*. Being able to relax properly is a gigantic problem because most people have no control over their minds. Proper relaxation, like everything else, has to be learned.

It is extremely important to realize that the body is a direct reflection of the mind. If the body moves, it does so because the mind moves first. All creation starts in the mind, whether it is negative or positive.

The truth is, people are what they *think* all day long. Like always attracts like, and a pessimistic attitude will not produce a happy, healthy, or successful situation. A thought that is low and negative will hardly ever rise above ground level, while a thought that is strong and positive can build wings of hope and fly to its highest destination.

Medical science shows us that every thought is an arrangement of chemicals in the brain, giving new meaning to the old adage "thoughts are things." By changing our thoughts, we literally change these chemicals in our brains, and that brings about changes in our lives.

Always practice an optimistic view of life and, in turn, life will perform at its best, bringing about a peace of mind and creating that sense of relaxation. We must learn to think, concentrate, and put forth all the necessary action required to achieve our goals, and forget about the things we do not want or need—including unnecessary tension. Through intelligent thinking methods, life is built, and through proper understanding and application, it is lived joyfully.

The mind moves the body, but the mind can also move itself. That is, the mind can be used to select and control its thoughts. If we do not like how our lives are going, if we do not like the stress and lack of relaxation, then we must change the underlying cause. We must change our thinking patterns. When this is done, slowly but surely we will see our lives changing right before our eyes.

Keep in mind that a complete change may take some time. We must learn to be patient with ourselves if results are to be what we desire. Remember how long it took us to get to this level in our lives. Depending on the situation we may be in, it could take just as much time to get on a more positive and productive level. But again, we cannot allow this to discourage us. If we don't at least begin, we will remain stuck—or worse yet, go deeper into our current problems and create even more stress.

Meditation can help in the adjustment to new thoughts and thinking patterns. Most importantly, to be successful meditators, we must realize that we are a product of our way of thinking.

Like everything else, becoming a successful meditator requires practice, practice, and more practice. With time, great results can be achieved. The more we do it, the easier and better it becomes.

Breathing Aids Relaxation and Creates Health

Becoming aware of our breathing during meditation is a good way to help us release idle thoughts and reach a state of relaxation. The breath is magical and serves a good purpose. It cleanses and nourishes our body internally. When the breathing is deep and slow, a person is calm and in control of the mind and emotions. When the breath is frantic and rushed, we find a rattled person unable to make the simplest decisions.

The breath and the mind are close friends in that the mind will follow the breathing. When the focus is on the breathing, the mind calms down, which helps to put us in the proper meditative state. When our minds begin to wander, we need simply to go back to thinking about breathing.

If at first we do not succeed, we must practice sitting still until we feel comfortable and relaxed. We will, of course, hear a voice that will try hard to convince us that there are better things to do with our time. This voice is very demanding and will try to weigh us down with excuses. Whenever we attempt to do something positive for ourselves, such as meditation, a part of our minds will take an active, opposite point of view. Be aware of this and do not give in to it.

Most people pay no attention to their breathing habits and feel they don't have anything to learn since they've been breathing all their lives. The problem is, most people are shallow breathers, using only the upper part of their lungs when they breathe. While that may be sufficient to keep them alive, it does nothing to increase their energy and their health.

We will not be truly healthy and feel good unless the body gets rid of wastes and toxins. The body has four major organs to remove wastes and debris—the kidneys, bowels, skin, and lungs. Every time we take a breath, we are pumping lymphatic flow through the lymph vessels. When we practice deep breathing, it helps to increase the removal of these wastes from the physical system through the lungs.

This brings us back to *ki* breathing. *Ki* is the primordial energy that flows through all things. By learning to breathe in such a way as to allow this energy to move through us freely, we will be able to cleanse and refresh our entire physical bodies.

We should think of our breathing not only as air going in and out, but as energy and life force moving through us. It is beneficial to energize ourselves as often as possible. Without this life force, the body will not survive more than a few minutes. We can survive weeks without food, and for several days without water. But just think how long we would last without air.

It's extremely important to realize and appreciate how proper breathing affects our overall well-being. According to Asian traditional beliefs, the kidneys play a major role in the body's energy. Deep breathing exercises charge these organs with this vital *ki* force. If a person is a shallow breather, the crucial systems in the body will not operate at their maximum level. When breathing is low, deep oxygenation of the body cells will be maximized, resulting in more energy and better health.

Ki breathing is an integral part of Aikido training. It is usually done in the sitting posture—that is, Japanese-style, with the legs folded underneath. If this position is a problem for an individual, a straight-back chair will do just as well. Sit straight in the chair with both feet on the floor with the hands resting lightly on the thighs.

This type of exercise requires the body to be in proper posture and alignment so the meridians are free and not blocking each other. Care must be taken not to slouch. The back must be straight but not stiff. The nose must be in line with the navel, and the chin lowered so that the back of the neck is comfortably stretched. The body is now in proper position and alignment, and one is ready to start the deep breathing exercises.

These exercises should always be done in a calm and unhurried manner. It also requires that a person concentrate on each exhalation and inhalation so that one can almost see each breath going in and out. Concentrating in this manner helps to block everything else from the mind and makes the action more powerful.

Ki breathing begins by exhaling through the mouth with the lips slightly parted and making the sound "haaah." It will sound like letting air out of a tire. Then exhale all the air out of the lungs slowly and deliberately.

Next, close the mouth and start the inhalation through the nose the same way, slowly and deliberately until no more air can be taken in. Hold this and make the effort to bring the energy down into the lower part of the body's center.

When exhaling through the mouth, the stomach muscles draw in. When inhaling, the stomach muscles are expanded.

Practicing *ki* breathing in this manner, in combination with the use of the abdominal muscles, is very beneficial to the body. The lungs, stomach, and other internal organs get a good workout. By prolonging the exhalation, stale air (carbon dioxide) is removed from the lungs. By inhaling deeply, fresh oxygen and energy are brought into the body. Deep breathing is one of the best methods for eliminating toxins from the body.

We need to realize that when we take a deep breath, it massages our internal organs and turns the air into energy which, in turn, improves our health. Deep breathing can help alleviate nervous tension and anxiety, reduce stress, combat insomnia, fear and panic, and totally revitalize our well-being, both mentally and physically. *Ki* breathing coordinates the mind and the body.

A black belt Aikido student who studied with me for several years disappeared one day. For many years, I did not hear from him or know of his whereabouts. One day, to my surprise, I received a letter from him thanking me for teaching him the *ki* breathing exercises. He wrote that *ki* breathing had actually saved his life.

After many years of alcohol and drug abuse, he had hit rock bottom and was on the verge of death. He began to drift in and out of consciousness. In desperation, he began to concentrate on the deep breathing that he had learned in his training. After three laborious days of deep breathing, he had removed enough toxins from his body to regain full consciousness and to begin his healing process. What a profound effect deep breathing had on him!

At the time of his writing, he had recovered completely and had not felt so healthy in a long time. He is now in hotel management and resides in San Francisco, California.

In the beginning, you can practice the *ki* breathing exercise for two or three minutes, then gradually increase the time as the endurance builds up. The longer it is practiced, the more energized you will become.

It is well to set a time aside every day when you can relax. This is the time to clear your mind of all thoughts and perform the breathing exercise. The best time is upon waking in the morning, since the air is fresher and the mind more receptive. However, after you become proficient, it can be done anywhere, anytime.

Try to develop the habit of taking a few deep breaths each time it comes to mind. This can be done at the office, driving your car, waiting for the bus, etc. Once you develop the habit of deep breathing and feel the results, you may find that you do not want to stop.

Summary

Meditation and deep breathing are nothing new and have been

practiced throughout the ages by many people all over the world. They are the means that will help an individual to link the brain, mind, and soul, and to experience oneness with the Creator.

In meditation, we have an excellent tool that can be used in our search for truth and spiritual development. Meditating properly brings about a definite connection to the higher intelligence which we call God. This helps us to see the areas in our lives that have to be changed and improved. We begin to realize what is important and what is not important regarding the choices we have and the decisions we must make.

In short, meditation brings about a clarity of mind and awareness of God's purpose for our lives. Just as the body needs food and water for survival, the mind and soul also need food—spiritual food that is derived from meditation.

Along with meditation, there is nothing like *ki* breathing. It cleanses, rejuvenates, and gives us the energy, strength, and courage to deal more effectively with life's ups and downs. It is a great tool for advancing one's self-mastery.

CHAPTER 8

Nutrition and Health

The body is a magnificent tool. If it is kept in excellent condition, it is capable of the highest level of operation. Nutrition and health are an important part of keeping the body functioning in perfect order so that the mind and heart can achieve a high quality of harmony and peace in all activities.

Nutrition and Health

Nutrition and health go hand in hand. We cannot expect our bodies to be healthy and strong and serve us well, any more than we can expect peak performance from our automobile if we pour cheap gas and oil into it and don't bother to keep it in good running condition.

Most of us never give a thought to our physical bodies and their functions as machines. Stop for a moment and make a comparison. There are some very interesting similarities.

Like a vehicle's motor, we need fuel, which comes from the food we eat and the water we drink. We have an electronic system to coordinate the mind and body in its directives and actions. The combustion engine needs the proper fuels delivered to the correct ignition points so there is a spark and compression at the right time. This intricate, wonderful motor will give years of faithful service when kept clean and cared for properly.

Beyond this, when our cars begin to malfunction, we either repair them ourselves or take them to a qualified mechanic to take care of the problem. A few worn parts may have to be replaced, or a change of oil and a general tune-up may be in order to get the car running smoothly again.

When the human machine becomes ill, we seek medical help to ease the pain and to help us get well again. In other words, we need a "human tune-up." The body sends out signals to let us know something is not right.

Learn to detect the warning signals in the body. We should know our bodies just as intimately as we know ourselves. We can get new parts for our cars, or perhaps we can buy a new one; but as humans we do not have that luxury in getting new body parts. Livers, kidneys, hearts, bladders, and other body replacements are not available in local parts stores. And when they are located, they are extremely expensive to install, with no guarantees that the body will accept the new parts.

Though our bodies may be compared to a machine in many ways, the greatest machine of all time is the first one that was ever made. It was made by the Greatest of the Great, the One we call God.

Man-made machines are totally mechanical in nature. They are made with many different parts that function blindly, and without consciousness or feeling. The human machine, on the other hand, made by God, has parts that are animated. They are conscious, self-moving, and, to a great degree, self-determining. The human mind has the power to choose and achieve something more than mere existence.

We humans have received a great gift from God with our human machine. It has a unique ability to heal itself with the proper fuels and care given at the right time. As long as we live in the physical body, it is wise to recognize its importance. Therefore, one must take a comprehensive look at the body and decide what essentials are needed to maintain the highest possible level of physical fitness.

The body is our wonderful servant and the sacred temple of our inspirations and desires. Care should be taken not to neglect it, misunderstand it, or drive it to death.

Eating Habits

Speaking entirely from a physical point of view, we are the result of what we eat, both of how and when we eat, as well as how much we eat. When we do not eat properly, our health suffers and it shows. We get frustrated easily, are short-fused, impatient, and anti-social.

Most people spend a great deal of time, energy, and money in acquiring a suitable home. They are proud to live in a clean, comfortable, and attractive home. They dislike the idea of their house being unkempt or dirty. They would not think of allowing anyone or anything to come into their house and mess it up.

The same approach and care should be taken with the body. The body is also a house—a house in which the spirit dwells. St. Paul referred to it as a temple, the "temple of the Holy Spirit." One must be very careful as the keeper of the temple and make sure it is kept clean inside and out. Do not allow anything to come in to contaminate it.

Cultivating the proper attitude in everything we do in life is of paramount importance. When we sit down to eat, we must have the proper frame of mind. Sometimes a business person in a café might be reading the newspaper while having breakfast or lunch. Nothing unusual about that, except that if the news is bad, mixing that with the meal may be quite depressing. This is not good for the digestion. When eating, take the time to taste and enjoy what is being eaten.

Meal time is a very special time, a time to be thankful for the nourishment that has been provided and is about to be consumed. There should be a sense of peace and quiet. Loud conversation, unpleasant business discussions, and serious reprimands should be avoided at the table.

It is best not to eat if the mind is upset, cluttered with fear or worry, or in a state of restlessness. Eating under such adverse conditions is detrimental to the health and a sure way to poison the system. It is best to miss a meal or two and wait until one is in a calm and relaxed state before eating.

Experts emphasize that food should be slowly and thoroughly chewed, since a large part of the digestive process takes place in the mouth before the food is swallowed. Many necessary nutrients are extracted from the food and absorbed through the walls of the mouth. Once swallowed, they are neutralized by acidic digestive juices, where part of the food potency is lost. Hurried eaters who do not chew their food well lose out from the vital nourishing absorption during the primary stage of digestion.

Eating incorrect mixtures of foods will also produce certain reactions that are harmful to the body. The popular Western practice of eating a large meal followed by dessert is not recommended by most nutritional experts. If we must eat sweets, it is best to eat them by themselves.

Another incorrect mixture consists of eating meats and dairy products at the same meal. Meat, being a strong protein food, requires powerful digestive enzymes for assimilation. By drinking milk, which is more easily digested, the meat enzymes are weakened, causing poor digestion of the meat, along with other distressing symptoms.

Liquids are not recommended with meals, since they also interfere with the digestive juices in the stomach.

Going a step further, indulgence of any kind is always a sure sign of lack of self-discipline and control. It is always better to eat less than too much. Overeating causes serious health problems. The body is overworked in digesting the food and is not given enough time to rest between meals. Quite often, overeaters are in fact suffering from malnutrition due to the intake of too many of the improper foods.

Overeaters are at a high risk for heart problems and numerous other illnesses related to weight. Not only do the body's appetites need to be wisely controlled, but restraint is an obligation that serves one's best interest. If unchecked or ill-managed, the body's appetites continue to demand attention even after they have been supplied. In this way, the body might be compared to a spoiled child who needs to be disciplined. The mind should be the master that controls the body. If the body's desires take control of the mind, the results can be disastrous.

On the other hand, replenishment is the law of life, and we suffer as many serious health consequences from not eating as from overeating. By not eating the proper food — that is, good clean nourishing food—not only do we die prematurely, but we suffer a great deal along the way.

The body must be supplied with the proper elements in order to have complete health and to function at its best. Good health is the basic foundation for the satisfaction of life.

Another problem that plagues many individuals is the search for the "perfect" weight-loss diet and an easy way of losing pounds. Countless books have been written about different diet theories. There are liquid diets, crash diets, and fad diets. Everywhere we look, we hear of someone who claims to have the ultimate secret to weight control or weight loss.

Unfortunately, the only thing we lose is our money, since most of these diets are worthless. I have personally known people who have gone on one diet after another for years without attaining the desired result of weight loss. We have become a country of followers in which the blind are leading the blind, simply because we have lost all common sense when it comes to the body and how to care for it in regard to food intake.

Many abuse their bodies by starving it one day and stuffing it the next. Others use excuses and tell themselves, "It is okay to abuse my body. This is Christmas, or New Year's, or my dog had a new litter." Often these same individuals consume enough food to give a horse indigestion, but sweeten their tea and coffee with artificial sweeteners or drink diet colas because they are watching their calories.

If we continually make excuses and remain on an unhealthy diet, we will prematurely kill ourselves. Many people have the attitude that they are going to die from something anyway, and thus they refuse to give up certain habits in life, because without those pleasures they feel life is not worth living. These people may be conscious of the poisons they are putting into their bodies, but the desire to change is not there.

While it is true that everyone dies from something, it is the *quality* of life that counts. Eating unhealthy food will not develop that quality in us.

Hazards to Health

In general, a lot of our food is so adulterated it is almost like eating plastic. We have lost the basics when it comes to nourishment. America is the most prosperous country, feeding half of the world, but it is also the most overweight and undernourished.

Ignorance is the major factor here. The public is not aware that the majority of diseases in our society stem from a combination of stress and inadequate diet.

Do not eat something just because it looks and tastes good. Body chemistry causes us to have various reactions to some of the foods we eat. Do a little research and find out what the food contains.

There are many good books that will help disclose the truth about the foods on the market today. As intelligent consumers, we should question what we purchase and whether it is proper for human consumption. In today's modern world, with all the advanced technology surrounding us, we also find ourselves surrounded by fast food places, instant and processed foods, artificial coloring, pesticides, and preservatives.

Pesticide-laden foods can cause much physical and emotional distress. Most of the time, we are unaware of the effects on our bodies. We ingest these pesticides through the eating process. Other pesticides are taken in through the skin. When we use indoor or outdoor pesticide sprays, our skin absorbs these poisons. Children are especially sensitive to pesticides which are used for the control of pests and insects, and also to chemicals in paints, sprays, and water purifiers (such as chlorine in swimming pools).

How can you start looking for the right foods, rather than buying what is offered on the grocery shelves? We most definitely have a choice, especially when it comes to our health. One of the first steps is to begin reading labels. We will find many long words that are meaningless to us, and we will also find words that will habitually turn up in many products.

Let's take an example: monosodium glutamate, better known as MSG. This is the sodium salt of glutamic acid, which is one of the amino acids that make up proteins and is also produced by the human body. It is important in human metabolism. Free glutamic acid occurs naturally in foods such as seaweed, tomatoes, and some cheeses. When these foods are used in their natural state in entrees, they have no side effects.

The synthesized form of MSG is made from starch, corn sugar, or sugarcane molasses, which may cause sensitivity in individuals by rapid absorption within the body. The risk arises when MSG is used in this concentrated form and consumed as a seasoning in prepared dishes. According to many reports, this flavor enhancer may cause adverse reactions such as headaches and drowsiness after eating, sometimes reacting severely in sensitive people.

This flavor enhancer has been widely used in the Orient to add to the flavor of prepared dishes. It is also found in most prepared foods such as canned soups, frozen foods, and candy. Food manufacturers use it for economical reasons.

Many restaurants use MSG in the preparation of their foods. However, due to the harmful effects it has had on many consumers, some restaurants will remove it from a person's entree upon request.

While MSG is no longer added to baby food, children may still consume it in other products used in their school lunches, such as processed or canned meats and fast foods. MSG is also present in mixes, convenience foods, and prepared foods served in airplanes, and even some "gourmet" restaurants. While the establishments themselves may not add MSG to their menus, many previously prepared foods may contain additives or related substances.

Hidden MSG is not limited to use in food. Sometimes it is hidden in soaps, shampoos, and cosmetics. One information source, *Truth in Labeling Campaign* (TLC), gives a list of products containing MSG.

Other foods are also hazardous to our well-being, such as foods that are artificially colored, baked goods that contain preservatives, and fruits that are covered with wax or sprayed with a chemical to speed up the ripening process and make them more appealing to the public.

Take a moment to consider that fruit, in its natural state, has no wax film whatsoever. It is sometimes not as attractive as waxed fruit with its shiny gloss. However, our natural temperature of 98.6 degrees is not high enough to melt the wax that is taken into the body. Therefore, after a period of time, problems may arise due to the wax buildup.

Beware of foods dyed to enhance their color. Alternative natural sources can be used for coloring without the harmful effects—dried beet juice, raisin juice, or cranberry pulp, to name a few.

Another culprit that has been found to cause allergic reactions is caffeine, which is found in coffee, colas, some teas, and chocolate. According to medical professionals, caffeine is a stimulant and affects the nervous system.

The mercury found in cans has caused health problems for many people. Sodium nitrite and sodium nitrate are widely used in cured meats and fish. It has been well established that these two compounds have caused human toxicity.

Many of the products mentioned here have been on the market for years. It is up to us to do research to find the truth of what we are ingesting into our bodies. If we think about the times when we did not feel well after eating a meal, we should go back and trace what it might have been that did not agree with the body's system, and avoid eating that particular food for a while. If the same symptoms return when the food is eaten again, we should eliminate the item from our diet entirely.

The foods that are most nourishing to the body are those in their natural state. If we look at our choices, we should buy organic fresh food instead of frozen or canned products.

Be more aware the next time you are in a grocery store. While standing in line, look at what others have in their shopping baskets, then look at the condition of their bodies. A picture is worth a thousand words.

Water

The best drink that can be given to the physical body is pure water. Nothing quenches the thirst better than a glass of sparkling, cool water. It has a cleansing and calming effect, besides keeping the physical plumbing in good working order.

Most of us have heard that we should drink at least eight glasses of water a day. Taken out of context, this simple statement is not totally good advice. We should drink plenty of water, yes, but it should be safe and clean, and fit for human consumption.

According to the universal consensus of most medical and health experts, our water supply is the most critical factor in our overall health. To date, more than 700 chemicals have been detected in U.S. drinking water. The E.P.A. has labeled over 129 dangerous pesticides and many toxic chemicals that are routinely found in tap water. These include bacteria, viruses, parasites, dissolved metals, asbestos fibers, pesticides, herbicides, and radioactive particles including fluorine and chlorine.

Dr. Bruce West, editor of the *Health Alert Newsletter*, claims that of all these, the major contaminants are heavy metals, chemicals such as pesticides, and chlorine and fluorine.

Water comes from two major sources: the surface and the ground. A standard system is used for purifying the water so that it is considered "safe" for drinking. The water is transported to storage areas where chemicals such as chlorine and lime are added to disinfect it. The water is then strained after the solid particles sink to the bottom of the basin. Chlorine is added in the final stage, among other disinfectants, to kill bacteria. Dr. West maintains that chlorine is particularly dangerous because it combines with organic material in the water to form cancer-causing compounds called trihaloinethanes.

While many water pollutants come from industries and businesses, the majority are put there by average citizens. It is not that people go out to the rivers or lakes and intentionally dump toxic chemicals into the water. However, some of our everyday behaviors have the same effect. Storm drains empty into rivers and lakes without being cleaned first, adding many toxins into the water supply. This includes lead that settles on the pavement from automobile exhausts, as well as automobile-related fluids such as gasoline, antifreeze, crankcase oil, brake fluid, and transmission fluid.

Other pollutants include seepage from septic tanks and underground gasoline tanks, animal waste, settled air pollutants, and fertilizers, pesticides, and herbicides commonly used on residential and commercial landscapes. The list is quite long.

Most city tap water is not fit to bathe in, much less to drink. It is the responsibility of each individual to help in keeping the water supply clean. We can do this by learning how to dispose of pollution-causing materials properly and not just dumping them on the ground, in the alleys, or down a storm drain.

Besides the contaminants that are already in the water, the drinking water has to travel through miles of filthy and corroded pipes before it reaches the tap.

The following information appeared in the *Dallas Morning News* in May of 1996:

> *The American Academy of Microbiology noted in a report last week that deteriorating water treatment and delivery systems pose a threat to public health.*
>
> *The poor state of water quality in general was the subject of a report released during the meeting. The American Academy of Microbiology, a leadership group within the microbiology society, warned that lapses in water treatment and delivery pose a threat to the health of the world's population.*
>
> *Even in developed countries, water systems are aging and deteriorating, a 65-member panel of scientists concluded. For example, in New York City some water pipes date to the late 1800s, said Rita Colwell, who heads the academy's board of governors. Without better investment in infrastructure, the public should expect more outbreaks like the 1993 Cryptosporidium epidemic in Milwaukee, blamed for 100 deaths. "It has become very obvious in the last year or two that we have a very serious problem," she said.*

For those who have no filtration system, a good practice is to run the water for about five minutes upon arising. This drains the lead and sediments that have settled in your house pipes overnight.

To date, water filtration is the best method of purifying water. There are three basic methods for this purpose; filtration, distillation, and reverse osmosis. The filtration system is composed of filters containing activated carbon or other filtering material, and are efficient in removing some heavy metals, pesticides, and other contaminants.

Distillation requires an electrical current to heat the water to steam. This method cooks the water and gives it a different taste. Most units are efficient, but expensive.

There are many types of carbon-filtering systems on the market today. Some are stand-alone units, and others can be installed onto the water supply pipes. One of the more popular methods is called "reverse osmosis." With reverse osmosis, water pressure forces tap water through a mechanical filter, which removes heavy metals and sediments. The water is then passed through a second-stage filter that removes micro-organisms and toxic matter. This is the filtering system used by industry in the purification of drugs and cosmetics.

Another alternative to getting clean water is to purchase purified bottled water at your grocery or health food store.

Take drinking water personally and do something about it. We owe it to ourselves and our loved ones to protect our health by drinking pure and safe water.

Alcohol, Tobacco, Drugs, and Other Excesses

Since drinking and smoking are accepted in many social circles, most people see no wrong in freely partaking of them. What happens when one abuses the physical machine by excessive intake of alcohol and smoke?

In recent studies, it has been reported that cigarette smoking is far more dangerous than previously thought. Researchers have reported that tobacco contains various chemicals, one of which is formaldehyde, which is extremely detrimental to human health.

There are no true studies or teachings anywhere that suggest the body machine needs alcohol or tobacco to run properly and operate efficiently. Inappropriate and intoxicating chemicals can cause the human electrical system to short out. The brain becomes numb, and the liver has to work extremely hard in its efforts to filter out the poisons. At some point, the human motor becomes tired and lifeless, and begins to balk.

Quite often, people will stop drinking and smoking when they are ill, or when their health is failing. However, when they are feeling well again, they ignore the warning signals and continue their indulgence in these dangerous chemical dependencies until the human motor has been fouled to the point of stopping altogether.

Smoking and drinking alcohol are not only harmful to us personally, but in the case of pregnant mothers, these harmful effects are passed on to the unborn babies. Some of these effects may also be transmitted through breast-feeding.

Drugs also can have undesirable effects on the body. Dependency on prescription drugs and over-the-counter drugs can produce serious side effects. Nowadays, a person grabs a pill as a source of immediate remedy. There are pills for this, pills for that, and pills for pills—thus throwing off an individual's balance and further taxing the body. Some people will not go to bed without taking a sleeping pill. Others reach for the aspirin bottle at the first sign of a headache. Still others depend on laxatives for their daily bowel movements.

People want instant relief instead of attempting to find the source of the problem. Pain and suffering are the consequences of what happens when man interferes with the normal functions of the body. We end up fighting ourselves rather than working to get the body back on the right track.

Other impediments to health include an excess of salt and sugar. There are pros and cons on the intake of salt, and moderation is the key. According to many nutritional experts, sea salt is a preferable alternative to table salt, as sea salt contains iodine and other minerals that are beneficial to the body. If we can reduce our consumption of both salt and sugar, we are better off since the body can get sufficient natural salt and sugar by eating enough fresh foods.

Sugar has hazardous effects on our children's health and, in excess, can cause major effects on their behavior. Sugar causes deterioration of the teeth and has been linked to hyperactivity in children. We often start our children's day with a bowl of boxed cereal loaded with sugar. We are poisoning their young and sensitive systems with empty calories that have no practical health benefits.

Sugar, in its natural state and in moderation, is not that bad. It is the chemical process that is used in whitening the sugar that is harmful. We must educate our children and demonstrate health patterns by example. Children can develop good eating habits for proper nutrition. It is a good idea to keep plenty of fresh fruit and vegetables, as well as fruit juice and good filtered water, available for their intake.

There are many substitutes for sugar, such as honey, maple syrup, barley malt syrup, brown rice syrup, molasses, and fructose, a derivative of fruit. By starting children on a healthier diet, they will soon lose their cravings for sweets.

What we eat affects our outlook in life. When we feel good, we are not so easily defeated by life's problems and frustrations. When we feel lethargic, we do not have the energy to cope with the simplest tasks, and we become very irritable. We want to be left alone. Our tolerance for others becomes limited, and the slightest things set us off. We lose our sense of humor, our patience, and sometimes our integrity.

Prevention

The most intelligent approach to good health is prevention. It is unwise to wait until disaster forces us to make changes in our eating habits. For those of us who are now blessed with good health, by all means we have a lot to be thankful for. But it should not stop there. We must continue to educate ourselves and find out how to stay healthy by eating correctly.

One positive step is to develop an exercise program. The sedentary life produces not only sluggish bodies, but sluggish minds as well. Get involved in a good exercise program. Start with a medical check-up, and, depending upon your age and condition, start on the path to good health. Keep in mind that the life of a couch-potato is not an exciting one. It is boring and unhealthy, and produces nothing of real value to anyone.

What we eat does affect how we think and how we act. Eat defensively and say "no" to certain foods like sugar, processed foods, and alcohol. The responsibilities and the results of how we nourish and care for our bodies are entirely ours. Eventually, the results of what we continue to ingest into our bodies will become evident. If the results are anything less than positive, we alone will suffer the consequences and have no one else to blame.

We all interact with germs and a polluted environment. Those with weak immune systems are more susceptible to illness than those with strong and healthy immune systems. While keeping the immune system healthy requires education and effort, it is extremely vital in fighting off disease and illness.

Our immune systems are directly affected by poor dietary habits, as well as by emotional and physical stresses. To protect and strengthen the immune system, we need to learn to avoid the elements that can cause harm and degenerative effects. Exposure to radiation and chemicals, chronic infections, drugs, alcohol, and tobacco abuse, as well as the lack of proper rest, all play roles in weakening the immune system.

With increasing age, the immune system also becomes less efficient at removing dead or defective cells from the body. There is a gradual decline in the ability to synthesize antibodies and protect cellular immunity. Good, clean food and water, as well as herbal and vitamin supplements, can be helpful in strengthening the immune system, along with exercise to keep the body strong and flexible.

In addition, to be healthy, the body should eliminate its waste naturally. Taking laxatives is far from the best solution. Constipation has been called "America's number one curse." Too much of the so-called good life, too much food—usually the wrong kind—and not enough exercise upset the body's natural balance and process. Laxatives often rob the body of potassium and are drugs we can live without.

This goes back to the law of cause and effect. Without resolving the cause, the effects will accumulate. Exercise and deep breathing help to massage the internal organs and help the elimination process.

Another good method to help eliminate toxic wastes in the body is skin brushing. Since one of the main organs of elimination is the skin, we can help eliminate toxins more readily by properly conditioning the skin through body brushing.

The benefits of daily body brushing are vital to good health. The skin protects our internal organs and easily absorbs outside matter and debris. It costs so little to care for the skin using this simple yet effective and natural method. All that is needed is a natural vegetable fiber brush that can be purchased at a health food store. Use long stroking motions three to five minutes per day. This should be done prior to showering or bathing, since the body must be dry. Removing the dry skin and debris is important so that it is not reabsorbed or does not clog up the pores of the skin.

You will feel revitalized as the waste and debris is removed from the top layer of the skin. Your body will feel alive as blood circulation improves and energy increases.

Any time we help our bodies eliminate toxins, we will feel an overall sense of improvement and well-being. Water and juices also flush the body's system of waste and acids as a preventive health care measure.

As creatures of habit, we have to correct damaging habits of eating, drinking, and also of thinking, in order to increase our health and energy. A craftsman selects the best tools and keeps them clean and in the best condition possible. Each of us should appreciate the importance of life and treat our God-given body with the same care and respect.

To achieve all this, a person may require a change in lifestyle. While change usually does not come easily to most of us—especially changes in a lifetime of eating habits—we still can find them exciting and much to our benefit. Change is necessary, because once we lose our health, we have lost the basic foundation for life's satisfaction. With good health comes good energy and a clarity of mind. Life's difficulties and problems become mere challenges to tackle and overcome.

As a result of my past lifestyle, I have been forced to make certain changes in my life, diet, and eating habits. I have consulted with numerous medics, osteopaths, chiropractors, spiritual healers, herbalists, health gurus, as well as a few quacks. Most of these people have something good and positive to offer, using different and various methods of treatment. Because of these experiences and research, I have devoted this lengthy chapter to diet and nutrition, which I regard as an important and essential part of our physical well-being.

Summary

The suggestions in this chapter should be viewed as guidelines. The author would like to make it clear that he is not an expert on nutrition. This information has been gathered by speaking with many nutritional experts and researching volumes of books on the subject of nutrition. Each person is different. What affects one person one way may not have the same effect on someone else.

However, we must realize that alcohol, tobacco, drugs, junk or devitalized food, as well as negative and excessive habits, rob us of personal power and the ability to develop our talents and perform at our best. We must learn to think for ourselves when it comes to what we put into our bodies and how to care for them. Do not be misled by false advertisements and social trends.

Try to cultivate a positive attitude in life and do not allow the mind to entertain negative and senseless thoughts. Remember that health is the first and most important asset we have. Learn to eat right and listen carefully to your body. It will let you know when it is not being treated well.

Remember, we are on the road to self-mastery, and this journey requires us to be self-responsible. We must take care of ourselves. No one can do it for us as well as we can do it for ourselves.

Epilogue

We are all passing through this world, and whether we realize it or not, we are all on a journey going somewhere. The primary question we should ask ourselves is not whether we want to go on a journey, but whether we are on the *right* journey.

We should ask ourselves three questions before we decide to take any new journey:

1. Where is the journey taking me?
2. Why am I going there?
3. What exactly do I expect from this journey?

These questions put us at a crossroad and give us an opportunity to determine a new direction. The trip, so far, has been one of trial and error, and we can depend on some of the things that have been learned as a result of past experiences to help us in the future. We have all attained certain levels of understanding and skill.

If we decide to begin the journey of self-mastery, we can become prospectors. We can make use of what we have learned in the past to make a better life at this time and in the future, not only for ourselves, but for all humanity. Strong consideration must be given to the consequences if we decide against going on this journey, as well as what that choice may mean to us later in life.

Getting started on the journey to self-mastery is actually harder than staying on the path once we get going. Remember, we cannot keep going if we never get started. All that we really need to do to get started is to make up our minds that we are going to do it. Once we start and begin to see results, the momentum will help pave the way.

On this journey, we will most likely experience many disappointments and frustrations. Sometimes we will feel as if we are spinning our wheels and not going anywhere. But we must hold firm to the knowledge that this road will lead to an important and rewarding destination.

Roads stand for progress and continuation. Unlike our pioneering forefathers who had to travel on rocky and dusty roads, we now travel on smooth superhighways. Imagine the hard work, pain, and cost in first clearing a path that served as a trail for their travels. The super-smooth roads we travel on now, and our ability to get from one place to another in a fraction of the time it used to take, is a direct result of the hard work and efforts of those who came before us. We, too, must put in time, effort, and hard work if we want to accomplish something greater in ourselves that will be a benefit for the future yet to come.

We must continue on the road to self-mastery in spite of obstacles. Some will try to discourage us by saying we are not on the right path, or that we cannot do this or that. In most cases, these individuals are not qualified to advise anyone on what they can or cannot do. They know little or nothing about us or about our capabilities. Often, those who try to instill fear and discouragement are small-minded individuals who probably never attempted or achieved anything of significance in their own lives.

Instead, listen only to those who have others' best interests at heart and who are in a position to help in a positive way.

The following list contains a few simple rules one can practice to help stay on the path to self-mastery.

- Develop a realistic and positive attitude.
- Monitor thoughts and feelings. Awareness starts in the mind.
- Learn to manage time well.
- Say no to time-consuming and distracting projects, social activities, and invitations that do not add value to your life.
- Be selective about friends and associations.
- Be selective about what comes into your mind through reading and television.
- Be selective about food and drink that is taken into your body.
- Learn to delegate responsibility. Find key dependable people to help with special projects, rather than overtaxing yourself.
- Acknowledge and show appreciation to those who show support.
- Do something nice for others.
- Resolve conflicting family, peer, or friendship problems by communicating. Speak clearly. Listen to the other person's point of view. Always add the ingredient of love.
- Take care of today. Yesterday is gone, and tomorrow may never come.

- Always set up contingency plans in case things do not go as planned.
- Keep clean and looking your best. Hygiene is very important.
- Allow quiet time every day for introspection, meditation, or prayer.
- Get proper rest, sleep, and exercise to regenerate the mind and body.
- Learn to laugh at yourself, and not take life too seriously.
- Develop a forgiving and optimistic view of the world.
- Be patient, but stay on the path. The results will be positive, and they will eventually come.
- Develop a strong faith in God and in y*ourself.*

The journey toward self-mastery is about life's lessons and learning. We need no special tools or permits of any kind. All we need is a strong desire to change our lives and become successful. Having a strong desire is the fundamental drive we need to get started on the path.

The person who knows about many things may be considered *learned*, but the person who knows what to do about those things is *wise*. Having knowledge implies that one does something with it. We learn by doing. Every avenue of discovery should lead to a time of action. Knowledge is power only if we put it to use. Mere knowledge is superficial: One either uses it or loses it.

The world is full of people with all kinds of degrees who, while considered to be brilliant, are pitiful failures in life. This is because they do not follow through with what they have learned. For example, many people go to church on Sundays to hear the Gospel, but do nothing about applying it to their actions at home and at work. The same can be said about many Aikido students who train only to learn techniques and acquire rank, but do nothing to apply the principles in their daily lives.

The process of learning is not complete until the knowledge has been applied and tested. The first level is to learn something, and the second level is to apply the knowledge. In the second level, one finds the value of the first level.

Like an old song says, "We are remembered only by what we have done." The passing world does not see our thoughts and ideas—that is, our knowledge. The passing world sees only what we are able to accomplish. That is, the passing world sees only our knowledge that was *put into action*.

There is no greater victory than victory over ourselves. With the victory of controlling the mind comes the realization that we need not be bound by fear and negative emotions. We can begin to sense the importance of peace and harmony with everything around us.

This is the achievement and purpose of Aiki. This is the goal of self-mastery.

ISBN 141201872-2

9 781412 018722